Joy Unspeakable

Contemplative Practices
of the Black Church

Barbara A. Holmes

Fortress Press / Minneapolis

JOY UNSPEAKABLE
Contemplative Practices of the Black Church

Cover art: *Over the Line* (1967) by Jacob Lawrence. © 2004 Gwendolyn Knight Lawrence / Artists Rights Society (ARS), New York. Used by permission.

Book design: Beth Wright

Library of Congress Cataloging-in-Publication Data
Holmes, Barbara Ann
    Joy unspeakable : contemplative practices of the Black church / Barbara A. Holmes.
        p.   cm.
    Includes bibliographical references and index.
    ISBN 0-8006-3643-0 (alk. paper)
    1. African Americans—Religion. 2. Contemplation. I. Title.
    BR563.N4H6536 2004
    248.3'4'08996073—dc22
                                                                2004011251

The paper used in this publication meets the minimum requirements of American National Standard for Information Sciences—Permanence of Paper for Printed Library Materials, ANSI Z329.48-1984.

Manufactured in the U.S.A.

Contents

for a praying mother and grandmother
Mildred L. Holmes
Mildred B. Schenck
for a loving father, who led by faithful example
Thomas (Talbert) Samuel Holmes

Preface

This book focuses on the aspects of the black church that point beyond particular congregational gatherings toward a mystical and communal spirituality not within the exclusive domain of any denomination. This mystical aspect of the black church is deeply implicated in the well-being of African American people but is not the focus of their intentional reflection. Moreover, its traditions are deeply ensconced within the historical memory of the wider society and can be found in Coltrane's riffs and Malcolm's exhortations, in the Step Brothers' dance routines and the fortitude of Thurgood Marshall.

Today increasing numbers of young people believe that the black church exists in a time warp, with slavery as its originating marker and civil rights as its culminating goal. Their history lessons have taught them that the black church is situated in a particular historical framework, but they also know that its traditions seldom include the concerns of a generation suckled on hip hop, "terror," and economic instability. Nevertheless, there is a timelessness at the center of black church practices that exceeds its history and deserves further exploration. I am speaking of a shared religious imagination that manifests as the communal intent to sustain one another and journey together toward joy despite oppressive conditions.

This book at first appeared to be a major change in the focus of my work. For the last few years I have been thinking about the cosmos and our place in it. From black holes to dark matter, I considered the cosmological aspects of Africana identity that were masked by discrete social and racial categories. Given the magnitude of these concerns and the work that is yet to be done,

I wondered why this new book was shifting my focus from the universe to the pew, from the galaxies to the hush arbors. As the writing progressed, I realized that I was grappling with yet another piece of the identity puzzle. Although the context in this book is congregational, the questions I bring to the task are familiar. Each of my books focuses on a taken-for-granted element of Africana life that has the potential to promote the flourishing of the immediate community and the extended family of God.

My first book was a study of prophetic proclamation in the speeches of Barbara Jordan, whose pragmatic discourses integrated religion, ethics, and law. Her willingness to "speak truth to power" from the liminal stance of black, female, segregated personhood elucidated the power of ordinary people to discursively carve hope from static and oppressive conditions. In *Race and the Cosmos*, I suggested that the languages of theoretical physics and cosmology could expand limited social constructions of identity, power, and race. In this book I am bringing contemplation into focus as an important taken-for-granted worship legacy in the historical black church.

I am also identifying the sacred territory of inner cosmologies and the spiritual locus of past microcosms of protection and communal formation. Those who study contemplation as a practice or religious experience soon find that they are engaging geospiritual spaces that have the potential to ease postmodernity's striving and disassociation. Perhaps through this retrieval of the contemplative practices of the black church, the trans-racial and diversity-based community-called-beloved will come into view.

The historical black church is the necessary matrix for this work. I am aware that the phrase "historical black church" can be problematic when it is used to gloss over complex and multifaceted worship choices. Accordingly, I am using the phrase as a cultural reference point that may illuminate or impinge upon a historical trajectory but is not limited to those disciplinary boundaries.

This book is a reflective turn toward practices that emerge out of the collective imagination of the worshipping community. I've named these practices "contemplative" (for lack of a better word) because they create intersections between inner cosmologies and the interpretive life of a community. The task is to reclaim the powerful interiority ensconced in the memories and practices of the historical black church, in the narratives of daily life, and in the vibrancy of Africana aesthetics. This is a legacy for future generations that must be identified before it can be bequeathed.

Communal contemplative practices in Africana contexts have been hidden from view by the exigencies of struggle, survival, and sustenance. As a consequence, there have been scant opportunities to reflect on the journey. But the time for reflection has come. What makes our future together possible is our ability to contemplate, to consider events and their meaning in narrative, cosmological, and historical contexts. I am suggesting that ensconced within the framework of vibrant religious practices are tangible reminders that our lives are communal liturgies.

We respond to a deeply interdependent and responsive universe through shared experiences. This means that despite signs of postmodern fragmentation and the rise of radical individualism, we cannot carve out shared destinies in isolation. We are born not only into a wondrous and mysterious life space but also into communities of interpersonal reliance. These communities of care and crisis lend meaning and congruence to our lives and help to shape our collective stories. These stories and learned practices disclose the pitfalls and potential for human fulfillment, but more important they describe a cosmos that is interwoven with mystery.

Unfortunately, we have few devices to handle the eruption of spiritual events into our ordinary lives. When they occur we are forced to reassess our taken-for-granted presumptions about the world. However, our assessments can further marginalize the events and those who claim to have them. If you listen to testimonies of immediate and personal spiritual experiences, you will inevitably hear "spectator" language that describes disruptive spiritual exotica. The presumption is that these moments cannot be easily interrogated and that they are not subject to the type of reflection that yields enlightenment or insight. Moreover, the impact of these ineffable moments on individual seekers further privatizes the religious experience in ways that undermine the interpretive power of a community.

By contrast, the communal contemplative practices of the black church provide an interpretive grid that synthesizes inner and outer cosmologies. It is the community and not the individual monastic that becomes the concern. The spiritual practices become public theology through acts of shared liturgical discernment. These acts of shared contemplation move individual mystical events from the personal and private toward the public and pragmatic. Accordingly, the inward journey transcends the private imagination to become an expanded communal testimony.

I am contending that communal contemplation is richer than the immediacy of personal experience because the experience, the story, the event is subjected to the gaze of both the individual and the community. In Africana and other indigenous cultures, this unique orientation toward the sacred elements of life begins at a very young age. Children soon learn that when events surprise, frighten, or mystify them, they can face the unknown with a discerning community. It has only taken a few generations to lose sight of this integral aspect of Africana community life.

Such losses can result from inclusion/integration into dominant cultural paradigms. The price for full acceptance is often cultural and spiritual amnesia. Moreover, communal contemplation takes focus, centering, energy, and concentration. These are orientations that tend to be displaced in the struggle for upward mobility. The price of inclusion turns out to be the loss of the communal reflective gaze, the interpretive moment, the pause for a fresh wind of the Spirit. It is this collective contemplative gaze in Africana contexts, worship, and community life that is the focus of this book. The contemplative practices of the black church are steeped in the stories of transcendence and transformation that have the potential to reinvigorate community life and to flesh out the character of black humanity with phenomenological detail and communal wisdom. I am offering an understanding of contemplation that depends upon an intense mutuality, shared religious imagination, and the free flow of interpretation within the context of a vibrant and lived theology.

Lived theology is a contextual and dialogical process that is always enhanced by a responsive and collegial community. I am grateful to the Louisville Institute for the General Grant that supported the research for this book and to Michael West, Beth Wright, and Fortress Press for their confidence in this project. I also want to acknowledge the Lived Theology project directed by Charles Marsh for initiating remarkable colloquies focused on experiential and lived theology. Rev. Nesbie Alston, Paul Dekar, Anthea Butler, Victor Anderson, Valerie Bridgeman-Davis, Stephen G. Ray, Cheryl Kirk-Duggan, Waldo E. Knickerbocker, Barry Bryant, Steve Edscorn, and many others contributed to the completion of this manuscript. Writing is a blessed wilderness experience. I am grateful for friends and family who journey with me.

Joy Unspeakable

is not silent,
it moans, hums, and bends
to the rhythm of a dancing universe.
It is a fractal of transcendent hope,
a hologram of God's heart,
a black hole of unknowing.

For our free African ancestors,
joy unspeakable is drum talk
that invites the spirits
to dance with us,
and tell tall tales by the fire.

For the desert Mothers and Fathers,
joy unspeakable is respite
from the maddening crowds,
and freedom from
       "church" as usual.

For enslaved Africans during the
Middle Passage,
joy unspeakable is the surprise
of living one more day,
and the freeing embrace of death
     chosen and imposed.

For Africans in bondage
in the Americas,
joy unspeakable is that moment of
mystical encounter
when God tiptoes into the hush arbor,
testifies about Divine suffering,
and whispers in our ears,
     "Don't forget,
     I taught you how to fly
     on a wing and a prayer,
          when you're ready
               let's go!"

Joy Unspeakable is humming
     "how I got over"
after swimming safely
to the other shore of a swollen Ohio river
when you know that you can't swim.
It is the blessed assurance
     that Canada is far,
     but not that far.

For Africana members of the
"invisible institution," the
emerging black church,
joy unspeakable is
practicing freedom
     while chains still chafe,
singing deliverance
     while Jim Crow stalks,
trusting God's healing
     and home remedies,

prayers, kerosene,
    and cow patty tea.

For the tap dancing, boogie woogie,
    rap/rock/blues griots
    who also hear God,
joy unspeakable is
that space/time/joy continuum thing
        that dares us to play and pray
        in the interstices of life,
it is the belief that the phrase
    "the art of living"
    means exactly what it says.

    Joy Unspeakable
        is
both FIRE AND CLOUD,
the unlikely merger of
        trance and high tech lives
        ecstatic songs and a jazz repertoire
        Joy unspeakable is
        a symphony of incongruities
                of faces aglow and hearts
                on fire
                        and the wonder of surviving together.

Introduction
An Unlikely Legacy

Oh, Jesus

The soloist moves toward the center of the podium. The congregation of about 1,500 breathes with her as she moans "Oh . . . oh . . . oh, Jesus." Those are the only words to the song. Unless you are sitting within the sound of her voice, it is difficult to imagine how a song of two words can be a cry of anguish, balm, and celebration. In each soaring note we participate in the unutterable spectrum of human striving. In this world you will have trouble but—"oh, oh, oh, Jesus." The shouts of exaltation give no indication of what is happening. Although it appears to be the usual charismatic congregational fare, in fact we are riding the stanzas through time to the hush arbors and swamp meetings, over the dangerous waters to safety. In this ordinary Sunday service something has happened and we are changed. The worldly resistance to transcendence that we wore into the sanctuary has cracked open, and the contemplative moment carries us toward the very source of our being.

Moments like this occur regularly in the black church, yet if you ask congregants about their "contemplative practices," they would be confounded. When I began this project, colleagues warned that there were no such practices. Despite numerous exceptions, black church worship is known for its heartfelt, rhythmic, and charismatic character.[1] This depiction has become such an accepted view that contemplative practices remain a subliminal and unexamined aspect of black religious life. As a consequence the practices are not nurtured, encouraged, or passed on to future generations. Yet when contemplative moments occur, worship experiences seem to deepen.

1

A Restless Longing

The experience that I have just described was not expected. The worship was inspirational; the singer was extremely skilled. Everyone present enjoyed the music, but there was more. In the midst of worship, an imperceptible shift occurred that moved the worshipping community from intentional liturgical action to transcendent indwelling. There is no way to describe this shift other than to say that "something happened." During this sacred time, the perpetual restlessness of the human heart was stilled and transformed into abiding presence. Time shimmered and paused, slowing its relentless pace, and the order of worship no longer took precedence for those enthralled by a joy unspeakable. The church where this service was held is Mississippi Boulevard Christian Church in Memphis, Tennessee, led by Dr. Frank A. Thomas. This church is unusual in that it has incorporated intentional contemplative practices into its worship services. The services begin with Holy Hush. As the people enter, they are encouraged to center themselves and pray. While the names of the sick and bereaved are read, the congregants, elders, and pastors circle and pray in small groups. At the end of the service spiritual leaders line the altar ready to receive those who need individual prayer and attention. This model of worship is no longer prevalent.

Today worship services move at such a pace that often there seems to be no space or time for the congregation to unify in spirit. In times past, the old folks would tarry, pray, and rest in the presence of one another until the lover of their souls joined them. Those elders who remember these Africana worship practices know that something is missing today. Perhaps *missing* is not the right word. As noted in my opening example, contemplative practices still exist in the Protestant black church, but they have not been consciously embraced and nurtured as necessary and important aspects of worship. The lack of contemplative abiding time creates a restless longing in the people.

Although I do not have the longevity of the elders, I have the same sense of absence. At first, I attributed my sense of spiritual incompleteness to the rigors of a lifelong spiritual quest and to faith needs that tend to be eclectic and complex. To complete the passionate weekly liturgy, I need moments of spiritual indwelling to be as integral to worship as the shout. Unrelenting praise teams modeled after cheerleading squads do not satisfy this need. Although there are many other religious traditions that value and teach contemplation, moving to one of these traditions is not an option for me. For some of us, church and culture are so intertwined in black church worship services that to leave one is to be cut off from significant aspects of the other.

Yet when I talk to other members of the black church community, I am struck by similar whispered concerns about this missing dimension. From religious scholars in the academy to lay evangelists in storefront churches, folks ponder the possibility of becoming "unchurched." Those who are unwilling to make such a drastic decision find themselves disengaging from the black church community as a last resort to resolve the emptiness that claims them as soon as they leave services for the parking lot. Some hop from church to church seeking and not finding, but most just accept the subtle spiritual changes as "a sign of the times." The ecclesial response to this complaint is that one must participate fully to get something out of the service. And so those who come desperately seeking often find themselves being told that their lack of fulfillment at the end of the service is their own fault.

I have no doubt that the church is as frustrated as the seekers. It yearns to fulfill the needs of the people but often uses tools that are no longer efficacious for the tasks at hand. The people are in pain; they are suffering from a kind of post-traumatic stress syndrome as a result of decades of denigration. Now that they are ostensibly free, they yearn to receive the "peace that surpasses all understanding," yet they may have preconceived notions of how the peace will come and where it will come from. All of these issues are hidden from plain sight, so that few realize that there is unhealed brokenness in every pew and pulpit.

The underlying bleakness of contemporary congregational life is masked by increasing technological advancements and business savvy in religious circles. On the surface, things have

changed for the better. At most black church services across
denominational lines, music is of professional quality, choirs are
uplifting and skilled, preachers are articulate and well-trained.
Yet the sense of centered belonging in a community that provides spiritual sustenance and intergenerational continuity has
become drastically attenuated. I am suggesting that this sense of
"centered belonging" can be located in the contemplative spiritual legacy of Africana people.

This legacy is particularly treasured and nurtured in Catholic
traditions. Although black Catholics also struggle for racial and
cultural inclusion, they have fostered and retained the contemplative aspects of their faith. Under the broad umbrella of black
church traditions, black Catholics also find their place. As M.
Shawn Copeland notes,

> black religion is an historical phenomenon *neither* Protes-
> tant *nor* Catholic, normatively centered in an African
> worldview, *even* if the language of its expression and the
> symbols of its ritual are Christian in inspiration and in fact,
> *even* if the very features of the Christianity peculiar to the
> enslaved peoples masked their Africanity.[2]

M. Shawn Copeland suggests and I agree that black religion is
characterized by its theological diversity and its broad spectrum
of cultural nuances. Accordingly, Catholic, Orthodox, Islamic,
and Protestant sources are important to this book. However, I
am focusing this study on the contemplative legacy of the Protestant segment of the historical black church, because it is within
this cultural bastion that the greatest losses have occurred. For
black Protestants contemplative practices are no longer within
the critical or reflective grasp of the community.

Contemplating the Invisible Institution

In days gone by, overtly contemplative events were not unusual
in black church congregations, who gathered for the specific purpose of evoking the presence of the Holy Spirit. Moreover, tran-

scendence was as integral to congregational life as the reading of announcements. When all were gathered "on one accord," the Spirit would descend upon the worshippers, inhabiting their bodies and lifting them out of the ordinary for a brief time. Today those moments occur less frequently in the black church.

At this point, it would be helpful to explain my usage of certain terms. I use the term *African American* to refer to the African diasporan community in the United States and the term *Africana* to denote Africans in various global contexts. The phrase *black church* is used in theological circles to describe many different aspects of Africana worship life; however, I am specifically referring to a dynamic religious entity forged in oppression and sustained by practices that were often covert and intuitive. All who have lived within its embrace know that the historical black church exceeds its walls, preachers, ideology, denominational focus, and Protestant/Catholic differences. Since we have just emerged from an era of activism, most would agree that the black church was crucial to the survival of Africans in the United States. However, I take seriously Delores Williams's distinction between the black church and African American denominational churches: "Contrary to the nomenclature in current black theological, historical and sociological works . . . *the black church* is not used to name *both* the invisible black church and the African-American denominational churches. To speak of the African-American denominational churches as the black church suggests a unity among the denominations that does not consistently exist."[3] Williams is correct. The black church has an actual and meta-actual form. It inhabits the imagination of its people in ways that far exceed its reach. Although it is no longer a truly invisible institution, it will always be invisible to some extent because it embodies a spiritual idea. This idea is grounded not only in history but also in the narratives and myths of an oppressed people. The black church has been a spiritual wellspring from the time of its origins in the hush arbors until it gave impetus to the Civil Rights Movement. In fact, for people of color the black church was one of the few safe spaces in an unsafe world.

The black church is in a sense "virtual" space created by the worship practices of the congregation. Over the years, the church has sustained, nurtured, helped, and hurt its people. It has been the progenitor of great triumphs but has also been the source of great angst, misogyny, homophobia, and confusion. Yet in all of its triumphs and failures, the black church has always been central to the life of the community.

Things have changed. African American communities and churches are not as homogeneous as they seemed during the years of sanctioned cultural oppression. Instead, both are becoming more diverse, and their needs are reflecting that shift. In North America, more black communities are centering their lives on secular ideals. The response of the black church has been to streamline its worship services, becoming more attentive to time expectations (length of services) and programming. Survival depends on the ability to keep the people attending and giving so that increasing budget demands can be met. Bible studies are less frequent than conferences led by star preachers, and worship music must compete with the professionalism of the music industry.

This is not to say that recent changes in worship are not a welcome improvement. We have all sat in a church where a squawking tone-deaf choir was excused because it was "inspired." Excellence in all things is a joy to behold. Because this postmodern era is characterized by a multiplicity of narratives and needs, the historical black church must identify and reclaim its diverse congregational practices and taken-for-granted spiritual gifts. The phrase *taken-for-granted* is familiar to phenomenologists; however, several crucial presumptions are encoded in the idea. Some internal aspects are taken for granted in the black church because they are intuitive, familiar, and inspired. This phrase takes on a whole new meaning when it reflects the presumptions of the wider culture about the practices of the black church. A common presumption is that black church worship practices are subsumed in liturgical enthusiasm and joyful expressions of adoration and praise.

Some of the charismatic practices, such as the dance, the shout, call and response, tuning of the preacher, and high-spirited choirs and praise teams, can be traced to cathartic religious expressions linked to the African continent. Others were sustained during slavery, and contextualized within the framework of an Americana spiritual ethos that emerged during the formative religious revivals of the Great Awakening and Azusa Street. While it is certainly true that cathartic and sustaining religious expressions predominate in many historically black congregations, these practices are only one aspect of a multi-faceted and rich tradition.

Indescribable moments of deep spiritual abiding bear all of the marks of contemplative practice, yet they are not identified as such in black Protestant churches. These abiding moments are so intense that once they are experienced, they are continually sought. Often the frenzied noise of a praise service is an attempt to recapture those defining spiritual experiences. Some of these contemplative practices bear spiritual traces of African indigenous religions but have developed particular diasporan elements in the Americas. African indigenous religions do not divide the world into rigid categories; instead, religion is deemed to be holistic and grounded in everyday life.

African indigenous religions tend to make few distinctions between sacred and secular, life and death, cathartic and contemplative. Instead, visitations from the spirit world are hosted, feted, or exorcised as the moment requires. In like manner contemplative moments in the historical black church were completely integrated into the life of the community. As a consequence, there seemed to be no need to highlight or amplify those moments, no need to preserve or bring these communal experiences to consciousness.

The question is whether the current generation will pass on a legacy rich in the diversity and complexity of the historical black church or whether one type of charismatic worship will obliterate all of the creativity we have inherited. I say this even though I am a Pentecostal deeply committed to evocative worship practices. Exuberance and social consciousness are only the most obvious contributions that the black church has to offer a history of human spiritual engagement. Moreover, when these charismatic practices are deemed to be the quintessential expression of black worship, our view of the black church is reduced to caricature.

The myth of unreflective joy is reinforced by the use of black worship to sell commercial products. One sees black church choirs and hears gospel music at political conventions and public gatherings and in advertisements for cars and fast food. Even as I write this chapter, a television commercial is presenting the "Sears Gospel Choir" joyfully extolling holiday cheer. One has to wonder what model of Christianity would allow this incongruous juxtaposition of images, practices, and ultimate goals.

My discomfort with commercialized uses of Africana worship traditions is exacerbated by the implicit respect given to other ethnic traditions. Although I am aware that advertisers have free rein in a consumer-driven culture and that very little is sacrosanct, I also note that I have never seen a Muslim cleric touting the detergent that keeps his robes fresh, orthodox cantors singing antacid ads, or an American Indian emerging from a sweat lodge with a name-brand deodorant in his hand.

Elders in the Africana community understood the value of communal worship traditions. Moses Berry shares his grandmother Dorothy's caution about carelessly offering precious communal wisdom to the wider world:

> If you share something sacred with people who won't respect it, they will try to reduce it to something that they can understand, and miss the sacredness. Therefore . . . don't let them know about your church music because they'll turn it into dance music or look at it like "folk music," and miss the point that it's the music of suffering people that lifted them from earth to heaven. It's not merely an art form.[4]

Grandmother Dorothy may be right. Reductionism seems to be the preferred hermeneutical lens of dominant cultures when they interrogate ethnic cultural practices. In many ways, Africana worship practices have been "understood" in the simplest of terms. My untested theory is that there may be a connection between the historical myth of the "happy slave," which sustained the crumbling conscience of a nation of slaveholders, and the "feel good" promotion of consumer products using the musical exuberance of the black church. Although participants in today's high-spirited televised depictions of black worship are ostensibly free persons within North American society, the commercial exploitation of their commodified glee in the electronic public square is evocative of times past.

A common assumption is that Africans in the Americas adopted Christianity in "childlike" and "simple" ways. This myth is perpetuated when studies oversimplify black church congregational worship practices or characterize them in very broad categories. Inevitably, change is described in the language of daunting cultural shifts—from slavery to freedom, from grief, separation, and oppression to unrelenting joy. These are Herculean conceptual leaps that do not reflect the inner struggles of the black church and its people. Moreover, these sweeping generalizations do not accurately reflect the incremental nature of liberation.

The consequences of such naive and cursory summaries of black life are far-reaching. Those who rely upon these inaccurate but commonly held social summaries of an entire group tend to believe that they "know" black people. They know how to enforce the law where "they" are concerned, and they certainly know the political inclinations and social proclivities of the community. When issues arise that require resolution, those who "know" the black community may be consulted instead of the stakeholding community. Even when the community is given an opportunity to speak on its own behalf, its message will inevitably clash with beliefs deeply held in the wider culture about its ambition, crime potential, and worthiness. Moreover, signs of discontent will often be dismissed as unjustified.

How can a community whose emotions are presumed to be transparent to the dominant culture be unhappy when "they have come so far"? To be understood as fully human includes the complex interaction of aberration, sin, and lament. In times past, the black church offered a multilayered response to suffering. When the mundane and the transcendent are interspersed in cotton fields and swamps, human responses will inevitably be varied. Yet this diversity is not reflected in current worship styles and practices. My need for this diversity is rooted in the contemplative practices many of us learned during childhood. Because this book speaks to the specificity of spirituality within the context of a discerning community, I offer for consideration the familial and social particulars of my own inward journey.

Confessions of a Front-Porch Anchorite

My entry into Africana contemplative practices began on the front porch of my childhood home. It is the porch and not the altar that connects me to the black church. The contemplative practices that I remember emerged from a loving, church-influenced but home-based operation. In the midst of a racially ambivalent culture, my parents developed a unique survival training that has sustained their children. They insisted that we develop interior as well as exterior connections to the Divine. They accomplished this by alternating cycles of contemplation and play into every day.

As children my sisters and I played among the morning glories and mud in the backyard of our multiple-family house filled with family only. In the afternoons we were required to shower, read, and sit on the porch like ladies in training, or like elementary-school anchorites. While other wild-eyed and fun-loving female peers rollicked with the setting sun, we fanned and scanned with bleary eyes dog-eared copies of *Bible Stories for Children*, *Coming of Age in Samoa*, and *Little Women*. My sojourns on the front porch taught me that meaningful spirituality required my full attention, that there might be times when mystery would descend and embrace me as an intoxicating surprise. However, during "ordinary" times the attention of mind and body was a choice I could make.

My parents were able to instill reflective practices in us because they also received the legacy of the contemplative life as a survival modality in their own context. My father was the son of Geechees, also known as Gullah people. They were rice growers transported to the Deep South from the coastal areas of West Africa, most probably Sierra Leone. Gullah people in the Americas have a particular religious history that is most visible to us in the praise houses on the islands off the coasts of South Carolina and Georgia. The contemplative practices of the Gullah (discussed more fully in chapter 3) include the ring shout and other communal gatherings that mediate mystery through a cultural sieve that prioritizes the pragmatic. Strangely enough, my contemplative inclinations were expressed most fully in the Pentecostal church. But that is the middle of the story, and this journey begins with the first step.

A Family Journey: Peril and Gifts

We are a family of storytellers. We always knew who we were because elders shared their "recollections" at the kitchen table. Stories include harrowing escapes, mysterious instances of divine intervention, and a matter-of-fact inclusion of personal achievements interlaced with visitations from the spirit realm. The story of our family's migration to the North is not unique, but it is particularly colorful. Most Africana families have migration stories that orally document the escape from peril as the realization of a spiritual exodus, envisioned and rehearsed by faith communities for many preceding decades.

Real and present danger was the impetus for my own family's migration to the North. They sacrificed much to flee. Escaping an overtly violent southland, moving to a covertly violent northland, my grandparents (on my father's side) were determined that their family would be protected from a society that was not safe for its darker members. The story passed down through the generations recounts a showdown in South Carolina between members of a deputized posse (that is, the Ku Klux Klan) and my father's family.

My father's family consisted of Holmeses and Thurmonds who owned their own land and were relatively self-sufficient until someone was accused of a social infraction in town. It is not clear whether a cousin forgot to lower his eyes when an Anglo woman passed or whether someone had spoken out of turn. In the retelling, the facts have become unimportant. What is important is the story of survival. It seems that my great-grandfather was warned that the offending family member would be taken in the night and "punished." The family decided to resist. They sent the women to the next town to prepare to catch the train north. Then the men lay in the field with their guns. Night after night they waited, until one night the Klan rode in, and the resistance began.

As the story is told, my great-grandfather and the other men shot everything that came in on a horse and fled to the next town, where the women waited. They thought that they were going to Michigan to a town named New Ark, where they might find work at automobile factories. But they were Geechees with heavy accents, and so their request was translated by the railroad ticket seller as Newark, New Jersey. And so it went.

I have wondered as I prepared this manuscript if lying in a field with a loaded gun, unsure as to whether you can prevail or whether you will be captured and burned alive or hanged, counts as a contemplative moment. Can you meditate when you leave the only land you have ever owned under duress? For that matter, in our own era what use is contemplation to a community besieged by drugs, violence, and materialism? When survival is the goal, can contemplative practices help? These are issues that are still to be resolved; however, my family's stories have convinced me that contemplation can occur anywhere—stained glass windows and desert retreats are not necessary. In fact, duress may facilitate the turn inward, the centering down that Howard Thurman identifies.[5] He says, "How good it is to center down! To sit quietly and see one's self pass by!"[6] During this moment of deep reflection, questions arise as to the nature of human existence and the deepest desires of the heart. Thurman continues,

> We look at ourselves in this waiting moment—the kinds of people we are. The questions persist: what are we doing with our lives? What are the motives that order our days? What is the end of our doings? Where are we trying to go? Where do we put the emphasis and where are our values focused? For what end do we make sacrifices? Where is my treasure and what do I love most in life? What do I hate most in life and to what am I true?[7]

This moral self-examination can take place in peaceful and safe surroundings or in crisis. In fact, when physical safety is not an external option, it becomes a priority to interior regions of the human spirit. If, as Peter Berger suggests,[8] we construct our own social reality, then that reality must be organized in a way that sustains all aspects of human life. We eat, sleep, and exercise to sustain the body. But how do we care for our spirits? The human spirit requires attentive listening prayer and an inclined will to flourish. But even when we are connected to an intensely vibrant interior life, unpleasant things will happen. The antidote to a life that is perilous and difficult is the continuing manifestation of "gifts" deemed to open conduits to the spirit realm and a belief in the manifest goodness of God's creation.

In Africana culture, good and evil are often deemed to be integral to the life space; no one is surprised when one or the other erupts unexpectedly. Those family members imbued with the gift of second sight helped to interpret those events. My Aunt Leola was one of the gifted ones, a contemplative who expressed her spiritual insights through dreams. For as long as I can remember, Aunt Lee had a direct link to the ancestors. She was born with the "veil," a thin membrane over the face of a child at birth that was presumed to alter their sight. While our perceptions are limited to three dimensions (time is the fourth), theirs reach beyond those limits. The ancestors would come to her and

tell her when transitions from life to death were about to occur;
they would warn her about problems, rejoice during family celebrations, and send messages to others in the family.
Although she received these messages in the privacy of a sleep
state, she brought the community into the discernment process
through the telling and retelling of the narratives. We did not
know it at the time, but her particular spirituality was quintessentially indigenous and African.[9] "African spirituality is based
on the assumption that life is influenced by relationships
between human beings and the visible and invisible forces."[10]
The emphasis on life as a continuum reminded each family
member of their connection to those who preceded them and
those who will follow.

When life is viewed from this perspective, community is no
longer an artificial construct but rather an organic system of
memory and responsibility. Although the experiential spirituality
that predominated in Gullah families often conflicted with mainline denominational religious paradigms, church was a necessary
aspect of family life. Formal worship helped to integrate faith
and experience with everything else, but did not supplant the
intuitive and creative religious responses or the memories passed
down through the generations.

Feeding Spiritual Hunger
On my mother's side of the family were slaves from the Maryland
Eastern Shore. They developed their contemplative practices
around meals. I can understand how people who work around
crabs and blue fish can develop spiritual practices that marry full
stomachs to piety. The informality of kitchen tables took the
place of confessionals. Important life decisions were made as
salmon cakes were rolled and collard greens were cut. Sunday
meals were open to any who wanted to come. Those without
families, those down on their luck would appear for the expected
fare. It was almost impossible to tell family from others by the
titles attached to their names. Aunts, cousins, and uncles were
often unrelated in the genetic sense but embraced and named as
family.

The men fished and brought their catch for these breakfasts that were almost always the same: clam fritters and fried fish, fried salt pork, biscuits, sometimes grits and coffee. There was not much money, but there was always a lot of food. My great-grandmother Susie Booker would always pray an inordinately long prayer over the food—so long in fact that the cooks would delay as long as possible, hoping that the late hour would shorten the prayer. Everyone knew that Grandma Booker had to take two trolley cars to get to church. If the hour was late, there was the hope that the prayer would be brief. She of course would pray even longer after prefacing the prayer with "I know what you devils are trying to do. If I'm late, I'm late."

Although one could find contemplative nuances in the communal prayers and everyday work of baking biscuits, it is in the legacy of the healers that I found the most overt practices. Aunt Rebecca (on my mother's side of the family) was a root woman. She cured the community with the herbs she collected in nearby woods. Her kitchen and living-room shelves were lined with jelly and mason jars chock full of medicinal herbs. Rebecca was the only one who knew which twigs and plants would fix what ailed you. After an initial diagnosis, a tea was prescribed, and whispered updates were passed after church. If the patient was not improving, another tea was offered. It was understood that the tea would only address the physical disorder and that sickness required healing of spiritual disorders as well. Prayers and intercessions took place as the herbal brew was prepared. Everyone knew when someone was sick, and so the healing process became the interest of all members of the community. Since there was no health insurance, no money for medicine or doctors, it was in everyone's best interest for Aunt Becky to succeed. And so a great deal of attention was lavished on the ailing person.

As a consequence, it is impossible to determine whether healings occurred because of the medicinal effects of the herbs or the solicitous concern of the community. On occasion, there were stories brought back from the "betwixt and between" regions where the ill dwell. These stories of a reality where healing became a tangible activity included their awareness not just of Aunt Becky's herbal ministrations and the prayers of the community but also of the spirits of the ancestors and divine messengers. Thus the community received spiritual witness to their beliefs about the multivalent aspects of reality and the multiple conduits to this transcendent space. In these small communities contemplation was an everyday practice that included nurture of the body and the spirit.

The lesson was that life was not to be lived as a truncated interlude without meaning. In the midst of a noisy secular life space, we were to know without question that the sacred far exceeded ordered Sunday worship services. The stories that I have recounted reinforced this message.

Whether contemplative practices emerged among family or church members did not really matter; our practices pointed beyond us toward ancestors and progeny. Whatever we were living through seemed to have its roots in "this too shall pass." Although our lives were grounded in the context of social and political realities, we knew that God was also present. Sometimes the indwelling was ritually invoked through liturgy and worship, and at other times the mystery arose in the midst of ordinary activities. We learned to embrace a spectrum of contemplative experiences in the most unexpected places.

I have not always been able to predict when these abiding times would arise. The places differ significantly and are only connected by my presence in the midst of faithful and expectant people. I have found myself in the midst of a transformative contemplative moment while worshipping with the Turkana in Northern Kenya, watching the procession of clergy and locals and the sounds of drums and hymns. Perhaps it was the heat or incongruity of regal African men in Scottish liturgical garb in the middle of the desert that created the sense of spiritual displacement; perhaps not.

I experienced similar moments on a hilltop in Sonoro, Nogales, Mexico, as we sojourned with a family in their cardboard and corrugated tin home. Time seemed to stand still as we ate dinner together in the darkened room. Outside, another "temporary" refuge caught fire and burned. There was no way to save the dwelling, so we stood and silently prayed. Similar moments occurred while singing "Amazing Grace" in a Japanese Christian church in Onjuku and while giving birth to my sons surrounded by strangers and loved ones. The times and places are less important than the shared experiences of holy abiding.

Bearing the Spiritual Imprint

I am a product of the black church and bear its spiritual imprint. Whether I am in a power suit, clergy garb, or shabby chic professorial getup, I cannot escape the power of the black church and its religious practices. Those practices connect me to a stream of life energy that surrounds and permeates my brief sojourn on this planet. And so I speak of the black church in ways that both conform to and occasional break the unspoken rules about such discourses. In the black community, talking about the black church is rather like talking about your mother. You can do it, but folk wisdom protocols insist that it must be done carefully and with respect. For me, the respect is inherent, but this stance is punctuated by occasional instances of rage, chagrin, and incongruous optimism about the church and its practices.

My concern is that the worship style of the black church is being homogenized into a blended ahistorical weekly event that bears no traces of its complex and diverse Africana origins. Instead, historical and spiritual origins are articulated as a single story of dislocation, oppression, resistance, and overcoming. Although this story was repeated throughout the generations as a testament to the survival of the community, basic aspects of the narrative have changed to support the myth of progressive attainment, and to justify the subsequent arrogance and classism of those who inherited "the dream." I am not alone in my concerns. Dr. Martin Luther King Jr. expressed a similar view. He said,

> Two types of Negro churches have failed to provide bread. One burns with emotionalism and the other freezes with

classism. The former, reducing worship to entertainment, places more emphasis on volume than on content and confuses spirituality with muscularity. The danger in such a church is that the members may have more religion in their hands and feet than in their hearts and souls. At midnight, this type of church has neither the vitality nor the relevant gospel to feed hungry souls.[11]

He goes on to describe a class-conscious church that tries to rise above its condition by creating a false exclusivity.

The other type of Negro church . . . boasts of its dignity, its membership of professional people, and its exclusiveness. In such a church, the worship service is cold and meaningless, the music dull and uninspiring, and the sermon little more than a homily on current events. . . . This type of church tragically fails to recognize that worship at its best is a social experience in which people from all levels of life come together to affirm their oneness and unity under God. At midnight [women and] men are altogether ignored because of their limited education, or they are given bread that has been hardened by the winter of morbid class consciousness.[12]

King notes the importance of a relevant and communal worship experience. At the same time, he rejects static worship forms that allude to cultural relevance but have none of the spiritual depth necessary for real sustenance. In the twenty-first century the survival of the black church community depends on its spiritual diversity. This diversity must be remembered, nurtured, and reclaimed. A first step toward this restorative act would be the retrieval of contemplative practices that began on the African continent and sustained the community during slavery and during the formation of the black church. Eventually the practices undergirded social activism and the secular arts.

Speaking of the Practices

This book seeks to provoke a critical conversation about the spiritual practices passed down through the generations that may sustain and nurture Africana communities in the future. I began to focus on practices after my own involvement with the Constructive and Lived Theology Projects and after conversations with religious historian Anthea D. Butler regarding her work with the History of American Christian Practice group. These discussions and experiences illuminated the theological potential ensconced in practices of faith.

Like many of the terms and phrases in this study, the word *practices* can be extremely elusive and opaque, reflecting only the expectations of the observer. Robert Orsi argues for a "hermeneutics of hybridity" that values the complex and diverse cultural appropriations of religious idioms. He suggests that "the key words here are *tensile, hybridity, ambivalence, irony*; the central methodological commitment is to avoid conclusions that impose univocality on practices that are multifarious."[13] Orsi's key words create a welcome space for Africana practices, because they are malleable and permeable concepts. Not only do these words provide space for innovation and creativity, but they also affirm the religious proclivities and experiences of ordinary people.

Theologies are not confined to designated sacred spaces; they also emerge in the mundane and in the midst of crisis. I am interested in the ways in which contemplative practices in the black church among laity reveal unspoken laments, embodied modes of survival and fatalism, and communal faith transactions. I am also interested in the ways that practices point to the future. If the black church is to respond to the intransigent social and spiritual problems of its community, it will need a greater variety and depth of worship options. I believe that one source of diversity and complexity is ensconced in contemplative spiritual practices. These practices are gifts received as the legacy of spiritual ancestors, the creativity of captured people, and the presence of an abiding Spirit. The "gifting" occurs at every stage of the diasporan journey and is remembered in varying degrees during years of displacement in the Americas.[14] The validity of cultural memory is the source of continuing scholarly debate. However, these debates are not focused entirely on Africana communities.

Africans are one among many groups that have suffered catastrophic displacement and oppression at the hands of dominant cultures. Other ethnic groups also document the pain of holocausts and forced migrations and are questioned as to the degree or veracity of their cultural memory.

I am reminded that human memory includes the accessible and the inaccessible. Some things can be easily recalled; other events are submerged in the collective and personal caches of consciousness. For Africans in the Americas, the Middle Passage was a traumatic journey, but it only took months—not years—for the captives to arrive. Imagine if you will that tomorrow you are bound and tossed in the hold of a ship with your countrymen and women. You may arrive at your destination months later sick, diseased, and bereft, but will you have suddenly forgotten everything you ever knew, every prayer and song? Or will those lost parts of your life be etched even more intensely into your consciousness? Oral traditions tell the story and yield a living history of contemplative worship rooted in an African reality.

The research for this book revealed a rich contemplative tradition that includes the legacy of European and African monasticism, a history of diasporan spiritual exemplars, and unique meditative worship practices that are evident from the first arrival of Africans in the Americas to the present. To unearth the contemplative possibilities that those experiences evoke, I listened to the stories of the elders, sifted through church archives, analyzed theological implications, and reclaimed my own Gullah roots. The Delta region of the United States and the Gullah Islands (coastal islands near Georgia and South Carolina) offer clues about the cultural roots of contemplation in the diaspora.

In these Deep South and offshore microcosms, Protestant contemplative traditions emerge from syncretically African practices. As we move forward from Africa and chattel slavery to the Civil Rights Movement, we find trajectories of contemplative consciousness throughout the social activism of the 1960s. During this era of transformation, the black church helped to translate private angst into public momentum.

Each of the chapters that follow sheds light on contemplative practices in Africana faith and worship. Chapter 1 focuses on a shared and divergent cultural history of Eurocentric and Africana contemplatives. In chapter 2 I explore the African monastic tradition and the indigenous roots of contemplative practice. Chapter 3 follows the slave ships from West Africa during the Middle Passage to uncover the inner and outer lives of slaves and the birth of a deeply contemplative "invisible institution."

In chapter 4 I discuss the emergence of congregational life and the unique contemplative practices of the Deep South. These practices range from the conversion experiences at the mourner's bench to the ring shout, chant, centering prayer in the hush arbors, church "shut ins," meditative dance circles (for example, sacred harp and shape-note singing), being "slain in the spirit," and tarrying at the altar. Here I consider the reclamation of contemplative congregational practices as a movement toward common purposes and communal restoration.

Chapter 5 uses Afrocentric midrashic biblical interpretation to reveal contemplative aspects of scriptural narratives as resources for sermons, prayers, and meditations in the black church. Chapter 6 examines the contemplative impetus in social activism and the spiritual and social contributions of contemplative exemplars like Howard Thurman, Martin Luther King Jr., Fannie Lou Hamer, and Rosa Parks. Chapter 7 follows the contemplative impetus into the world of "secular" music and entertainment. In the Afterword I summarize the discussion and consider the tasks ahead.

Where from Here?

In an era of subliminal rather than overt racial tensions, the black church searches for a way to heighten its relevance to members and nonmembers alike. Whereas the twentieth century will be known for the cataclysmic clashes over social justice and communal liberation, twenty-first-century urgencies may include issues of alienation and moral fulfillment. Identification of African American contemplative practices and the lessons of individual and communal mediation of the divine may provide the resources for congregational and spiritual renewal.

Since the Civil Rights Movement wound down and equal opportunity for all became the prevailing social presumption, the Africana community in North America has been hurtling toward destruction and transformation. I suggest these two sociospiritual destinations not as polarities but as a motley mix of undifferentiated possibilities that tug the community "every which way but loose." Every gain is seeded with just enough destruction, personal and communal, to deflate and nullify the sense of accomplishment. Likewise, each failure is tattooed with the ancestors' hope and determination to overcome all obstacles even in the midst of abandonment, crime, and the skewing of moral values.

In the face of current dilemmas, we continue to hurtle toward the phantom goal of integration, a goal that was never an option in the first place. To be certain, the desire to prove self-worth and wipe out a history of oppression in one generation has taken its spiritual toll. The weariness I encounter is so pervasive and so deep that it cannot be assuaged by the usual liturgy and shout. Something more is needed in the spiritual lives of Africana communities. I am proposing that this "something" must include a healing reclamation of a unique Africana contemplative heritage—its communal rituals and practices, both silent and oral.

Retrieval and recognition of African American contemplative practices will enhance existing Africana worship traditions, expand spiritual options for an increasingly diverse community, reconnect diasporan contemplative practices to the broader contemplative tradition, and increase awareness of the rich diversity in the black church. The church is a living organism. It ebbs and flows with the pulse of congregational life and tends to reflect local cultural and spiritual realities. Essentially, churches grow at the direction of the Holy Spirit, being attentive to the needs and calling of the community of faith.

I am concerned about the life and future of the black church because of its monothematic approach to worship. I want black congregations to embrace crucial spiritual linkages to contemplative practices that give its membership access to a greater variety and depth of spirituality. Although the exuberant and charismatic tradition will always be a valued part of Africana worship traditions; the contemplative legacy is equally important to the faith and life of these congregations. In fact, the most profound contemplative moments may be ensconced within the very practices that have been identified as charismatic. Just a sigh beneath the organized exuberance of postmodern black worship, just a moan away from the rock/soul/gospel trend is a treasure of contemplative history, practice, and communal worship that is crucial to the survival of a people who bear the psychic and emotional scars of unresolved angst and oppression.

Retrieving this legacy is important because we can no longer assume that the tradition will be passed down through generations of church-going families. Increasing secularization in the African American community and the increasing diversification of faith options make it imperative that the stories and practices be retained. But even more crucial than the retention of practices is the healing of the wounds of generations past.

1
Contemplation
A Cultural and Spiritual History

The intense approaches to God . . . of the Shekinah, which is
our driving force, are linked with indescribable joy.
        —Jürgen Moltmann

We are not merely the ones we know or believe ourselves to
be. We all can leave ourselves; we are all able to be different
and to immerse and transcend ourselves.
        —Dorothee Soelle

Contemplation is sustained sympathetic, reverent attention. It
is what occurs when we take time to dwell.
        —Ronald L. Grimes

It is good to make an end of movement, to come to a point of
rest, a place of pause. There is some strange magic in activity,
in keeping at it, in continuing to be involved in many things
that excite the mind and keep the hours swiftly passing. But it
is a deadly magic; one is not wise to trust it with too much confidence.
        —Howard Thurman

In a world where cell phones ring incessantly and internet
hookups are active 24/7, who has time to dwell? Soelle, Grimes,
and Thurman describe practices that seem totally out of sync
with postmodern lifestyles. And yet faith communities continue
to use the language of prayer and intercession as if interaction in
transcendent realms is expected and possible. Among Christians,
the biblical story is one of intimacy and relationship. It is a story

that dares its adherents to live into the surprising mandate to be neighborly in a world that may not reciprocate. It is a call to inhabit multiple realities and human-divine possibilities. But how does one enter a space where Spirit and flesh can wrestle and embrace?

Contemplation seems to offer one possibility. As Grimes notes, contemplation invites us to enter into "beingness," into a space where listening, repose, and receptivity predominate. In such a space, anything is possible. This chapter engages contemplation as a cultural and spiritual phenomenon and as a manifestation of spiritual intimacy in European and Africana contexts.

Defining Moments

Although meditation and contemplation are often used interchangeably, there are differences. Ernest E. Larkin, O.Carm., describes meditation as "active prayer, discursive in method, in the control of the practitioner and available to all persons of good will."[1] Larkin's presumption of "control" is curious given the context. Few explorations into the inner recesses of humanity and even fewer conversations with God through prayer or meditation remain within human control. I think of meditation as a reflective process, a thoughtful engagement with text, Spirit, and religious experience. M. Basil Pennington describes *meditatio* as the repetition of sacred words and phrases.[2] This repetition invites the soul and spirit into a deeper union with God.

In the black church, repetition is integral to the ministries of music and preaching. Rhythmic discursive cues invite congregants to ride repetitions into the inner sanctum. By comparison, contemplation implies a spiritual repose that is still attentive and faithful. Larkin agrees and in a more personal way describes contemplation as

> knowledge by way of love, the fruit of a search, the experi-
> ence of God's love poured forth in our hearts by the Holy
> Spirit . . . the experience of what God is doing in my own
> being in Christ. It is what is left over in my body, soul, and

spirit as the aftermath of my meditation. There are moments of contemplation in every meditation.[3]

Larkin uses the words *contemplation* and *meditation* interchangeably at times, but points to specific definitional nuances that invite open-ended and creative spiritual practices. These practices beckon earthbound bodies toward an expanded receptivity to holiness. But what do we mean by the word *holiness*?

Certainly, holiness is a concept that makes ordinary people nervous. Perhaps the uneasiness occurs because the word implies a certain level of impossibility. But it also alludes to the potential danger that someone might dictate behaviors or impose their politicized theological attitudes on others. Such efforts are usually an attempt to conform human frailty to the likeness of a holy God by any means necessary. The holiness that Jesus describes has less to do with pious character traits and more to do with the hosting of God's abiding presence. It is not effort but invitation that opens the human spirit to the possibility that God may sojourn with us.

Reflective apprehension is not a cognitive exercise but rather the involvement of intellect and senses in a spiritual reunion and oneness with God. When this oneness occurs, it is accompanied by heightened spiritual awareness and insight. Contemplative moments also carry with them the potential for mystical encounter, which only compounds the difficulty of describing the experience in words. C. S. Lewis's attempt to explain his own mystical event is a prime example. He says, "I felt as if I were a man of snow at long last beginning to melt. The melting was starting in my back—drip-drip and presently trickle-trickle. I rather disliked the feeling."[4] His wry comments are clearer than any somber attempt to describe the event with exactitude. Rather, this contemplative moment is a spiritual event that kisses the cognitive but will not be enslaved to its rigidities.

An Interfaith Heritage

Our twenty-first-century ideas about contemplative practices are borrowed from a Christian heritage that relegates contemplation to desert mothers and fathers, anchorites and monastics. Although we have learned much about contemplative experiences from our Catholic brothers and sisters, there is a rich but neglected legacy in the Protestant tradition. When the word *contemplation* comes to my mind, I think of Thomas Merton and his lengthy and illuminating discourses about the practices that include complete dependence on God.

But I also want to talk about Martin Luther King Jr. and his combination of interiority and activism, Howard and Sue Bailey Thurman and their inward journeys. I want to present Sojourner Truth, Harriet Tubman, Fannie Lou Hamer, Barbara Jordan, and the unknown black congregations that sustained whole communities without fanfare or notice. Like Christianity, contemplative practices come in many forms; these practices have survived and thrived through inculturation and ethnic adaptation. This is how Howard Thurman describes the embodied locus of contemplation:

> There is in every person an inward sea, and in that sea is an island and on that island there is an altar and standing guard before that altar is the "angel with the flaming sword." Nothing can get by that angel to be placed upon that altar unless it has the mark of your inner authority. Nothing passes . . . unless it be a part of the "fluid area of your consent." This is your crucial link with the Eternal.[5]

Thurman's metaphors emphasize mystical aspects of the journey inward but also focus on the free-will decision to embark. To my mind the most promising aspect of the description is the impenetrable sanctity of the inward sea. This island is a bastion of interiority, a safe space to encounter God. External oppression may defeat the body and perhaps even the mind, but the inner sanctum will not be breached without consent. As I see it, the human task is threefold. First, the human spirit must connect to the Eternal by turning toward God's immanence and ineffability with yearning. Second, each person must explore the inner reality of his or her humanity, facing unmet potential and catastrophic failure with unmitigated honesty and grace. Finally, each one of us must face the unlovable neighbor—the enemy outside of our embrace and the shadow skulking in the recesses of our own hearts. Only then can we declare God's perplexing and unlikely peace on earth. These tasks require a knowledge of self and others that only comes from the centering down that Thurman advocates. It is not an escape from the din of daily life; rather, it requires full entry into the fray but on different terms. Nor is his call to pause and rest an admonishment against ecstatic practices.[6] This activity can be silent or evocative, still or embodied in dance and shout. Always contemplation requires attentiveness to the Spirit of God.

In this regard Jürgen Moltmann agrees that when we respond to our internal leanings toward divine reunion, we are always engaged with God's *Shekinah* glory. Moltmann describes the Shekinah's activities by saying that "even in our most frightful errors, it accompanies us with its great yearning for God, its homesickness to be one with God."[7]

According to Moltmann, "the Shekinah is not a divine attribute, it is the presence of God. . . . But it is not God in [God's] essential omnipresence. It is God's special, willed and promised presence in the world."[8] He further contends that the Shekinah does not leave us but exults when we connect to the God who so loves us, and wanders with us when we strive to escape divine destiny and embrace. Life is a journey: even when we try to remain in a static and unchanged condition, we are moving in one direction or another—closer or further away from God. In every culture this movement reflects the innate desires and greatest fears of the people. And so, inevitably, their practices are varied, rich, and informative, and their spiritual leaders are diverse.

From the experiences and narratives of ordinary people, we learn that contemplation is often a conduit to multiple realities. Accordingly, the effort to identify contemplative practices in the black church must include an interdisciplinary and interfaith approach. For this reason, Catholic dialogue partners, Islamic mystics, and indigenous traditional wisdom repositories are important to this Protestant study. These dialogue partners have been intentional about nurturing and retaining contemplative spiritual practices that open the human spirit to the heart of God writ large in the universe.

Contemplation is a spiritual practice that has the potential to heal, instruct, and connect us to the source of our being. Thomas Keating describes the shift in reality structures that may occur during contemplative prayer in this way: "our private, self-made worlds come to an end; a new world appears within and around us and the impossible becomes an everyday experience."[9] This paradigm shift has real effects in ordinary life, particularly for communities in crisis. Since crisis is one of the contexts for the emergence of the historical black church, one would expect to find thriving contemplative practices in its history.

Escaping the Boat of Habit

In Africana contexts, religion and ordinary life blend in such a way that specific practices are often the most tangible experiential indicators of the contemplative moment, the movement from ordinary time to transcendent indwelling. Because these moments are illusive, I will describe one process of contemplation that is based on the work of Howard Thurman and Basil Pennington. I have divided the contemplative experience into three accessible categories: entry, engagement, and effect.

Entry denotes a shift from the everyday world to the liminal space that worship creates. As Keating notes, contemplative practices facilitate a transition from the everyday world to an altered reality. Because the portal to this "other world" is never located in the same place, and because the experience is usually so intoxicating, it is not unusual for congregations to adopt intensely emotional worship techniques in an effort to reenter this space and re-create previous experiences.

The preaching moment offers another moment of entry but not for the reasons that most preachers assume. Rhetorical prowess, dramatic enactment, and storytelling may act as distractions as well as conduits to indwelling. The portal opens when word, song, or movement melds with the internal knowing and recognition of those who participate. When the invisible chord is plucked, the everyday socially constructed world recedes and joy unspeakable unfolds. However, entry requires a relinquishment of control, which can be both an obstacle and an aphrodisiac in Africana contexts. Those historically divested of all power do not relinquish it easily. In the days of hard labor, potlicker, and pork scraps, there was little to lose. It was a gift to enter into the complete abandonment that worship offered. Now, with vestiges of economic power and the desire for upward mobility, entry into a space of listening and reunion is a challenge.

Engagement refers to the willingness to involve body and spirit in the encounter with the Holy. It is upon this ground of covenantal reciprocity that relationship becomes paramount. Common experiences during the engagement phase may include an altered, disassociated, or heightened sense of reality or mystical encounters that defy the limits of language. During engagement, participants may be ecstatic or silent. When silence is the vehicle for contemplation, it differs significantly from the silence that is marked by withdrawal and absence. In the black church silences are interactive, malleable, and often punctuated by the vocalizations of those who are in various stages of contemplative focus. During these times, sounds are not interferences; rather they are guides to those on the contemplative journey.

However, engagement also evokes trepidation and avoidance. Those who have been traumatized by oppression may be uncomfortable with reflective and meditative activities. To survive, one must inevitably stow feelings, dysfunction, and myriad other "healthy" responses to systematic abuse. Those who have buried these issues in the center of their souls are not anxious to participate in activities that will bring the memories and pain back to consciousness.

Effect is often specific to the participating person or community. Those caught up in this intimacy with God explain that the experience expands their knowledge, awakens a palpable and actionable love, and is either a profoundly restorative resting in divine presence or a "fire shut up in the bones" that inspires action. The action can be restorative of personal relationships or proactive for the needs of the community. As William Shannon writes,

> the paradox of the contemplative way . . . involves a darkening and blinding of the exterior self and an awakening and enlightening of the inner self. The time comes when it is necessary to darken and put to sleep the discursive and rational lights that one was familiar with in meditation. This is no easy task, for one tends to feel guilty about relaxing and resting in the darkness; and there is a strong inclination to climb back into the safety and security of the boat of habit.[10]

As it turns out, the journey inward is not just a pious excursion for people of African descent; it is the embrace of all that has become antithetical to dark people. In my book *Race in the Cosmos* I focused on the scientific analogies that reinforce the power and pervasiveness of darkness.[11] The disassociation with darkness as the price of assimilation has alienated dark people from its restorative potential. Shannon introduces the possibility that darkness may be the blessed dimming of ego-driven striving, a destination and condition of safety and repose. In this state of trusting refuge, the light of divine revelation, which pierces but does not castigate the darkness, may finally be seen.

Entry also presumes that contemplation changes lives. There is a saying in the black church that "we don't want to worship out of form or fashion," and yet a "going through the motions" type of worship is surprisingly prevalent. The test of effective worship is not the fervor in the songs or the trance and dance; it is in the "fruit" or evidence in the lives of those who enter into joy unspeakable. I saw evidence of the lack of fruit in a large charismatic congregation. A preacher one Sunday suddenly stopped the order of worship to ask the person who had cocaine in their pocket to come up to the front of the church and throw it on the altar.

In charismatic circles this is called "word of knowledge," because it is presumed that the Spirit informs the speaker of information that they have no way of knowing. While I do not discount this possibility, it is also possible that some mother had spoken to the preacher of the day about her child's drug habit; perhaps this information was dropped into the preacher's consciousness as she was preaching. There is no way to know. However the results of her call to repentance was shocking. Within moments, the altar was filled with people throwing drugs on the altar. The pastor expected perhaps one addicted person to respond; instead hundreds began to file down the aisles. They kept coming until it became necessary to stop the videorecording. The same people who only moments before had been dancing holy dances and shouting were living lives that did not reflect their worship style. The environment that allows cocaine and charisma to share space during worship confounds the spiritual imagination. Somehow prophetic proclamation and worship fervor had become disconnected from the very essence of committed and faithful practices.

Clearly, the answer to these disparities will not be found by layering contemplative practices over familiar rituals. The situation that I described could only occur where worship is a thin veneer over life struggles that are not moored to faith-based ethics. The people coming down the aisles needed something that they had not received in the dance and the shout. Perhaps they had needs that could only be met by a reflective turn toward the stillness at the center of the universe.

The Early Years:
A Shared History of Christian Contemplation

Contemplation is one of Christianity's many threads. From the beginning, Jesus' ministry modeled the interplay between prophetic utterance, public theology, and intense spiritual renewal. He launches his three-year ministry from the desert wilderness, a place that will be the home of latter-day desert mothers and fathers. After an intense time of fasting, testing, and submission to the leading of the Holy Spirit, Jesus returns ready to fulfill his calling. These rhythms of activism and contemplation, engagement and withdrawal resonate throughout his life.

As for the early church, its origins are steeped in the intimacy of close communal groups in house churches and catacombs. During the first century, Paul refers to the knowledge of God as an understanding that exceeds rational and objective thought. This knowledge can be experienced as presence. The prophets and wisdom literature celebrate the accessibility of this presence and extol the mysteries of the human/divine relationship. Theological contemplation usually assumes the tangible reality of God's love, our shortcomings, and the inexplicable possibility of reunion. Accordingly, relationship is a primary goal of Christian life.

This willingness to engage God through a devout community of committed individuals is a theme repeated in many religious communities. However, the specific Christian mandate to "be in but not of the world" seems to be the necessary orientation that fosters and encourages connections to the multiple realities of faith. Persecution only strengthened the tendency toward a life that emphasized interiority as well as liberation. The era of persecution, which occurred during the formative years of the Christian church, also spurred the development of contemplative practices.

We are familiar with the story of persecution and martyrdom in early Christianity. However, we are not as familiar with the history of persecution and martyrdom (Anno Martyr) in the African Christian church at the hands of Emperor Diocletian. Those who went silently to their deaths include Saint Sophia, Saint Catherine martyred by Maximus, and Saint Damiana, who was killed with the other devotees in the monastery that she founded.[12] As most historians note, the end of public persecution marked the shift in Christian status from a beleaguered sect to the state religion of Rome.

When Christianity began, it was small and intense, communal and set apart, until it found favor with the state. Those adherents who witnessed Rome's public affirmation of Christianity in the fourth century realized that the contemplative aspects of the faith could not be nurtured under the largesse of the state. And so in the fifth century monasticism flourished in the desert as Christian converts retreated for respite and spiritual clarity. Although the desert mothers and fathers sought harsh and isolated sites, they soon found that they were not alone. The decision to retreat drew others to them. Communities formed as city dwellers came out to seek advice and solace. The historical model of contemplation offers the rhythm of retreat and return. It was in the wilderness that African contemplatives carved out unique spiritual boundaries.

Monasticism and Africana Legacies

> For too long, little or no honor has been paid to those who laid the foundations in Africa for the preservation of Christianity throughout the world. . . . The roots and headwaters for this monastic flourishing had their source in African soil. Unfortunately black saints have been depicted as white and African bishops have been portrayed as Europeans. The remembrance and acknowledgment of our historic spiritual foundations is long overdue.[13]

Paisius Altschul's complaint is well-grounded. African participants in the early church remained in the shadows of main theological discourse despite the scholarship of Tertullian, Augustine, Cyprian, and others of African descent who were instrumental in the expansion and theological grounding of the early church. Although initially the spread of Islam limited the expansion of North African Christian practices to sub-Saharan Africa, the trajectories of today's Christian contemplative practices can be traced to early Christian communities in the Middle East and Africa.

Some of these communities were led by women.[14] Yet for many years I did not make the connection between my own childhood home-based contemplative experiences and the origins of Christianity, which evolved in similar ways. After Christianity became a state religion, the freedom that women found in Spirit-led Christian sects was foreclosed by an increasingly hierarchical religious structure. In response many retreated to remote desert areas to continue their spiritual quests.

> The desert may initially seem barren, dull, and colorless, but eventually our perceptions start to change. . . . Here we empty ourselves of our own obstacles to God. In the space of this emptiness, we encounter the enormity of God's presence. . . . The ammas teach us that the desert becomes the place of a mature repentance and conversion toward transformation into true radical freedom.[15]

If the desert is a place of renewal, transformation, and freedom, and if the heat and isolation served as a nurturing incubator for nascent monastic movements, one wonders if a desert experience is necessary to reclaim this legacy.

One need not wonder long when there are so many deserts within reach. Today's wilderness can be found in bustling suburban and urban centers, on death row, in homeless shelters in the middle of the night, in the eyes of a hospice patient, and in the desperation of AIDS orphans in Africa and around the world. Perhaps these are the postmodern desert mothers and fathers. Perhaps contemplative spaces can be found wherever people skirt the margins of inclusion. Perhaps those whom we value least have the most to teach.

We are in need of those values central to African monasticism and early Christian hospitality; they include communal relationships, humility, and compassion. Laura Swan sums up these virtues in the word *apatheia*, defined as "a mature mindfulness, a grounded sensitivity, and a keen attention to one's inner world as well as to the world in which one has journeyed."[16] Inevitably, the journey takes each of us in different directions; however, by virtue of circumstances or choice each of us will at some point in our lives find ourselves on the outskirts of society listening to the silence coming from within. During these times, we realize that contemplation is a destination as well as a practice. The monastics knew this and valued both.

The period of individual monasticism in Egypt and Ethiopia gave way to the founding of schools of theology. From the twelfth century through 1517, when Martin Luther led the schism that would ultimately begin Protestantism, mystics—such as Saint John of the Cross (1524–1591), Saint Teresa of Avila (1515–1582), and others—kept the European tradition of contemplation alive. Along with this identification of contemplation with spiritual exemplars came the presumption that the contemplative life was reserved for professional clerics or solitary individuals gifted by God in intensely mystical ways.

In the effort to return power to the people, European Protestant reforms attempted to translate the mystical elements of contemplative life into issues of character, virtue, and a stalwart work ethic. In the process some of the soul delight was lost. Eventually, contemplative moments in Protestant worship occurred only during prayer time. When prayer became a public ritual rather than an intentional personal and communal practice, connections to historical contemplative practices gradually lost their centrality. Occasionally Protestant contemplative communities emerged, such as the deaconess communities led by Lutheran pastor Theodor Fliedner (1800–1864) and Waldensian communities started by Peter Valdes (circa 1140–1217) in France.

In more recent times, the Sisters of the African Brotherhood Church in Kenya formed a Protestant contemplative community in response to the catastrophic effects of missionization on the Kamba tribe.[17] The forthcoming work of missiologist Paul Dekar will highlight the contemplative history of Holy Transfiguration Community, a Baptist community in Australia, which began in 1970.[18] However, these formal Protestant contemplative communities tend to be the exception rather than the rule.[19] Most Protestants of European descent distanced themselves from contemplative practices as they distanced themselves from the Roman Catholic Church.

Roman Catholic church historian Waldo Knickerbocker suggests that the erosion of contemplation in Protestantism has a variety of causes, including the rise of nominalism in the late medieval period with its emphasis on an epistemology that has reason as its primary component, and the intense focus on the "particular" (individual) rather than the "universal" (community).[20] Knickerbocker proposes an interesting route toward the restoration of Protestant contemplative practices. He suggests reflection on theological and embodied meanings of the Trinity. According to Knickerbocker, prayerful reflection upon the reality of God's relationship to Spirit, Son, and humankind draws the supplicant toward the deep waters of contemplation.

Knickerbocker also highlights the role of Mary as a contemplative exemplar and recognizes the role of African theologians in this process. He says,

> An African father of the Church who played a major role in guiding the church in understanding all of this is Cyril, patriarch of Alexandria in the early fifth century and a major leader in the Council of Ephesus (431). It was at Ephesus in the doctrinal statement of 433 that the Church acknowledged Mary as *Theotokos* (*Mater Dei*, Mother of God). This was confirmed in the Chalcedonian Christological Definition of 451. In doing this the Church was acknowledging Mary's "pondering" epistemology, which includes her contemplative way of knowing.[21]

Apparently, the Protestant church has many options for reclaiming its contemplative heritage through exegetical interpretation and cultural appropriations; however, the first task is to remember that we have forgotten.

While it is true that European Protestantism neglected its contemplative roots, this legacy has fared no better in Africana contexts. The reasons differed, but the results were the same. In African American communities, the cost of integration and assimilation was the submergence of mystical traditions and ritual practice beneath Anglicized worship styles. Because people of color embodied difference, they wanted to "normalize" all other aspects of their lives. The intent was to mirror the dominant culture and their public and private proclivities so as to bolster the presumption of humanness. Since humanness and whiteness were deemed to be synonymous, Africans in the Americas avoided public ritual divergence. To this day we talk about the inculturation of Christianity in African contexts even though it has only been partially contextualized in the African diaspora.

Inculturation: Creating a "House" of Their Own

For most western Africana communities, the Middle Passage emotionally and intellectually contributes to a sense of displacement. Despite historical accounts of thriving Christian communities in Africa and the faith contributions of African church fathers and mothers, slavery is seen as the great Christianizing force in North America. The effect of this presumption is that there is no intense need to retrieve African Christian religious history that preceded the Middle Passage. Moreover, the legacy of racism is so subtle and so pervasive that even in seminaries church historians seldom mention the African origins of famous church leaders.

The use of ancient city names and locales helps to obscure information that would connect the black church to these ancestors. I have seen maps that locate Tertullian and Augustine in the northern section of Africa in such a way that the majority of the page is assigned to the sea. Only the boundaries of continents are visible around the edges of the page, making it impossible to identify the continent of Africa as the geospiritual origin of many church fathers and mothers. As a consequence, only the most curious and persistent students will pursue the issue. Old Testament scholar Randall C. Bailey makes this salient observation:

> When one looks at maps of the "Bible Lands" one confronts the same tendency of de-Africanization. In other words most maps either show only Syria-Palestine or that region

and areas to the east. If there is any depiction of Africa it is usually restricted to Egypt . . . but that often omitted the African nations of Cush, Put, Cyrene and the like.[22]

It is clear that "until nearly the end of the seventeenth century, Africa remained, for Europe, little more than a coastline, and for that matter a coastline not very representative of the interior."[23] This reluctance to attribute historical contributions to Africans is exacerbated by the fact that Christianity was never translated into the African consciousness even during its origins. Northern Africa was a Latin bastion of the church, without any semblance of inculturation. On this point, Louis-Vincent Thomas and René Luneau offer the following:

> African Christians had never been given the opportunity to be genuinely "at home" in Christianity—a chance to live in it as a house of their own, which they might on an ongoing basis through the contributions of their particular talents. The reasons for this state of affairs are inscribed in history. How could a church that had swept in on the coattails of colonial conquerors fail to seem . . . a foreign world?[24]

While Thomas and Luneau correctly point out the lack of African inculturation of Christianity on the continent, what they fail to note is that inculturation is never an act of total displacement of previously held ideas. The possibility of living in Christianity as "a house of their own" would necessarily include the continuance of indigenous belief systems. Africans were not likely to supplant one belief system with another. Religions were layered one upon another, and then they were tested for their efficaciousness. Throughout African history, indigenous beliefs coexisted with Islam and Christianity. If a certain emphasis developed, it was because a particular faith system seemed to improve the lives of the people. Conquerors could only affect surface practices; the prioritizing of religious allegiances remained with the people.

Theologian Stephen G. Ray Jr. subsumes this problematic legacy by suggesting that Africana Christian faith has been treated as an interloping reality in the stream of religious history. This racial bifurcation of perceived Christian origins creates reluctance on the part of African Americans to claim John Calvin, Luther, and John Wesley as mentors in the faith, while members of the dominant culture are unwilling to acknowledge their connection to African church fathers and mothers, Augustine, Tertullian, and Saint Mary of Egypt. Ray concludes that we share a common history with rich cultural elements that enhance our common origins. He urges the church to reject the cartography of race that severs Christian history into white and black discourses.[25]

It is not only race that separates Africana people from a rich contemplative tradition, but also the failure to retain our stories. One reason that church history and its recall of Africa's contemplative heritage have not affected the black church in any meaningful way is the pain that history carries with it for Africans in the diaspora. Few are willing to look back more than a few decades; most elders will not share the stories of "hard times coming up." Some communities even protest exhibitions of slave artifacts because of a diffused sense of cultural humiliation, and none of the contemporary Hollywood movies about slavery (for example, *Amistad*, *Beloved*) has been a commercial success in black communities. Moreover, the lives of ancient bishops and apostles are so far removed from hip-hop culture and the striving of black "buppies" that these icons of the faith lack relevance for black congregational life.

At this point in the discussion an important question arises. If there is a "disconnect" between the African origins of the early church and the historical black church, then what model of Christianity is being followed? Certainly, many Christian expressions and practices in the black church emerge from experience and creativity. But the black church also operates out of a constructive cultural amnesia still clinging to remnants of the malignant forms of Christianity offered by slaveholders. This is not Christianity at all but may be what William R. Jones refers to as a creative and adaptive form of "whiteanity." Jones describes this religious legacy as a subliminal virulence that threatens the spirituality of Africans in the Americas.[26] This is a powerful indictment and one that must be considered. The legacy of

Christianity does not begin on the plantation: it starts with the beginning of the Christian story, continues through Pentecost and the Roman Church, then spreads throughout the world. When this history is reclaimed, contemplation can be seen as an integral aspect of Africana faith and practice.

Scholars continue to wrestle with the issue of white Christianity and the authentic spiritual lives of Africans in the Americas. One of the most recent to do so is Josiah Ulysses Young III, who declares the humanist arguments of Anthony Pinn in *Why, Lord?*[27] and the theodicy postulates of William R. Jones to be theoretically sound. Yet Young is unwilling to fully accept their conclusions; as he says, "I don't believe Christianity can be reduced to the white man's religion."[28] Young contends that the problem lies with "a racist interpretation of the gospel rather than the gospel itself."[29]

If Young is correct, the gospel encodes myriad spiritual pathways for all to discern, even if some of the malignancies of racism remain a subliminal element in ecclesial structures and traditional interpretations of Holy Scripture. But how are congregations to plumb the depths of God's will through these infested denominational hierarchies? I am suggesting that inculturation is not enough; rather, experiential returns must be included in the process. Contemplative practices provide the linkages that Young and others overlook; they provide concrete and identifiable links to African spiritual traditions. While it is true that some of the practices are lost, others survived intentional and neglectful eradication and are enfolded into familiar Protestant black church rituals without acknowledgment. Black congregational life offers a diverse mix of faith traditions but also needs to identify its history, its forerunners and leaders, its fatal attraction to assimilation, and the powerful potential of its hidden contemplative practices to restore the broken commonweal.

Comparing Traditions

The key to contemplation in the black church seems to be its emergence as a communal practice. Although European mystics and contemplatives often lived in community, they tended to focus on the individual experience of encountering the divine presence. African American contemplatives turned the "inward journey" into a communal experience. In this ethnic context the word *contemplation* includes but does not require silence or solitude. Instead contemplative practices can be identified in public prayers, meditative dance movements, and musical cues that move the entire congregation toward a communal listening and entry into communion with a living God.

Spirit possession was sometimes but not always marked by physical and vocal expressions. Sometimes at the mourner's benches, the prayer shut-ins, or the humming of baptismal or communion music, the community ascended together to that "third heaven" that Paul enigmatically describes. Then in the midst of the dance, the song, or the spoken word, the community entered into joy unspeakable, a contemplative experience shared by the congregation.

This communal approach to the contemplative tradition is not unusual given the testimony of the apostles. As William Johnston points out, "all through the Acts of the Apostles, we find the Spirit descending on the *group*, communicating gifts and *filling all* with [God's] presence"[30] (emphasis added). In similar fashion, the African American church developed rituals and practices that nurtured and encouraged congregational encounters with the mysteries of God. Always the focus was on piercing the veil between secular and spiritual realms through shared experiences.

Although Africana and European Christians share a common contemplative history, there are specific differences in expectation and practice. Contemplation in Africana contexts differed significantly from the European tradition. It often bore the mark of the shout, dance, and meditative faint ("slain in the spirit"). In Eurocentric contexts contemplation and silence were presumed to be synonymous. Unfortunately, the pervasiveness of this presumption helps to shroud the emergence of contemplative practices within the vibrant and ecstatic Africana traditions.

In fact, contemplative history seems to include communal and individual expressions, ecstatic and silent worship. In Africana traditions, the desert mothers and fathers offer one model of contemplative practice; the songs of Alabama chain gangs at the turn of the century, the rhythmic chants amid cotton rows in Mississippi during slavery, and the murmured hymns of domestic workers offer yet another. Those of us who grew up and worshipped in historically black church congregations wonder how a religious tradition that values bodily spirit possessions and performative vocal entreaties to a personal God can be considered contemplative.

The answer is hidden in plain view and is ensconced in historical presumptions about the boundaries and practices of contemplative worship. If the model for contemplation is Eurocentric, then the religious experiences of indigenous people and their progeny will never fit the mold. But if contemplation is an accessible and vibrant response to life and to a God who unleashes life toward its most diverse potentials, then practices that turn the human spirit inward may or may not be solitary or silent. Instead, contemplation becomes an attentiveness of spirit that shifts the seeker from an ordinary reality to the *basileia* of God.

There are many similarities in Afrocentric and Eurocentric approaches to contemplation. They include focused piety and devotion as well as an individual and communal commitment to the spiritual life. The cultural differences between Afrocentric and Eurocentric approaches to contemplation include diverging concepts of human-divine relationships and the connection between daily life and divine action. These differences are exemplified in the discussions of the contemplative life by Catholic theologian Thomas Keating and Egyptian desert father Saint Moses the Black. Keating describes contemplation in ways that merge and diverge with beliefs in the black church. Although he rejects the mysticism that is central to contemplative practice in Africana contexts, he describes the experience of resting in the Spirit as "a mild suspension of your ordinary sense faculties and you slip to the floor."[31] "Mild" is an understatement. In the black church the contemplative experience is sought as an intense melding of spirit and body that changes the life of the community and the individual. In a chapter that describes what contemplation is not, Keating lists most of the experiences that characterize contemplation in the black church. Historically Africana communities did not value the "self-made world" of radical individualism. The community was the undisputed lynchpin for individual and group cohesion. Whereas some forms of European contemplation expect the unseen world to integrate spiritual enlightenment with personal autonomy and rationalism, Africans inculcated the unseen world, the world of the ancestors, and the interplay of spirits into everyday life. Desert father Saint Moses the Black describes the purposes of monasticism as "purity of heart."[32] This state of being is offered as the ultimate purpose of human life. Saint Moses reminds us that we often stray from this path during the life journey. I understand his entreaty to be a focus on holiness. Saint Moses seems to seek a simplicity of spiritual focus in the Jesus tradition. He refers to this purpose as "the carpenter's rule," a spiritual plumb line that will guide the seeker.[33] Where issues of purity and holiness are concerned, the traditions are closely aligned; however, extreme divergences seem to occur around the issue of silence.

Is Silence the Issue?

Any new ontology must take account of the historical expressions of all cultures . . . whose silence expresses a fundamental ontology of both objectivity and intimacy. It is a silence which may no longer terrify us, and it is a silence which in its showing might give us an understanding of the human mode of being which moves us beyond conquest, enslavement, and exploitation. In acquiring this understanding, we may recover the patience and the sensibility which lie at the heart of a religious attitude: "Be still and know that I am God."[34]

Those who study contemplation have assumed that the difference between European and Africana approaches to contemplation is based on the presence or lack of silence. This distinction could only be made during the modern era, as historically silence was interwoven in both traditions. Although silence is not necessarily the focus of contemplation in Africana contexts, it is always a part of the human experience. We tend to presume that one must create silent spaces for contemplation. It is as if we have drawn the spiritual veil around contemplative activity, seeking to distance prayerful and reflective practices from the noise of the world.

Charles Long speaks of silence as a way of being. He uses colonization as an example and contends that European domination in Africa and in other nations elicited the silence of those captive cultures. However, despite the imposed silences, these cultures did not cease to exist; instead they signified their ontology through myths and symbols.[35] Long alludes to the power of silence but warns that "it is difficult to get at the meaning of silence, for though a kind of power is signified through its quality, the power of silence is so unlike the power of words that we have no words to express it."[36] In Africana contexts, this may mean that ineffability is translated into dance or song. Accordingly, an ontological silence can occupy the heart of cacophony, the interiority of celebratory worship.

There is always an available language, whether it is drum talk or the mumbled laments of the stricken. Max Picard makes a salient point when he describes his understanding of the true nature of silence:

> Silence is a basic phenomenon . . . a primary, objective reality, which cannot be traced back to anything else. It cannot be replaced by anything else. There is nothing behind it to which it can be related except the Creator. . . . Silence is a world in itself, and from this world of silence, speech learns to form itself into a world. . . . Real speech is in fact nothing but the resonance of silence.[37]

Picard recognizes silence as the source of all being, the connective substance of ontology. Each spoken word carries silence on the horizon of articulation. Silence is the mediator of meaning and also our home. For as Picard notes, we live between the silence that we are born from and the silence that we go to in death.[38] Accordingly, silence is the sea that we swim in. Some of us allow it to fully envelop and nurture our seeking; others who have been silenced by oppression seek to voice the joy of spiritual reunion in an evocative counterpoint.

Reclaiming a Contemplative Tradition

The history of contemplation includes the creative contributions of Africans in the early church. Those who lived in the house of Christianity without making a home set up mimetic responses to Eurocentric traditions that influence current worship practices in the black church. Others chose the wilderness and carved out monastic interpretations of God's call for radical obedience and love. Still others emerge from mystical Islamic traditions. The black church has a contemplative history and a unique communal spirituality. This treasure can not survive on the shallow tendrils of slavery; instead it requires recognition of deeply connected roots to the early church, its creative syncretism with other faiths and cultures, and African indigenous responses to the sacred.

Ahistorical people are at great risk. They tend to fill the void of intergenerational connections with noise and activity. As Thurman so aptly notes, we cannot fall prey to the busyness that is a deadly magic. As frightening as it may be to "center down," we must find the stillness at the core of the shout, the pause in the middle of the "amen," as first steps toward restoration. Contemplation in Africana contexts is an act of communal reflection and reflexive engagement with both knowable and unknowable occurrences. In communal settings, it is the confluence of atomistic experiences and reflections grounded in a shared interpretive process. This communal contemplative legacy of Africana communities is a living but subliminal legacy with roots in ancestral traditions on the continent of Africa. The next chapter explores these traditions.

2
Retrieving Lost Legacies
Contemplation in West Africa

We have to return to the past to see what remains of the present.
  —Sankofa proverb

How sad that you yourself veil the treasure that is yours.
  —Mowlana Jalaluddin Rumi

Something occurred in Africa that was so deep, so powerful, and so rich that it affected the rest of the world.
  —Paisius Altschul

African religions have neither founders nor reformers. They have neither "authorized versions" nor canonical scriptures. The religions simply flow out of the life of the peoples.
  —Henry H. Mitchell

Africa, My Africa

The Africa that I turn to for the roots of indigenous contemplative practices is as much a construct of my diasporan imagination as it is the object of my historical interest. Few Africans in the Americas have visited the continent, and even when we do, we encounter the specifics of localized culture that only give us hints about the broader context. My visit to Kenya cannot help me to unravel the intricacies of Senegal. On a continent as ethnically and religiously diverse as Africa, there is little that can be generalized. However, one can discern unique cultural orientations.

Today many people rely upon Discovery Channel footage of secret ceremonies for their view of Africa. Is it any wonder then that Africana contemplative practices have completely slipped from view? In this chapter I explore the indigenous practices that speak to the African contemplative spiritual legacy. I am particularly interested in the practices of West Africa because it is from these shores that most of the diaspora began the Middle Passage to the Americas.

Also, I am grateful for the research of African scholars. In recent years our glimpses of African life and worship have been greatly enhanced by the scholarship of John Mbiti, Muse Dube, Joseph Olupona, Marcel Oyono, Jean-Marc Ela, and Mercy Amba Oduduye. Their research points to a cosmology that embraces multiple realities without clear demarcations between everyday life and the spirit realm.

In West Africa, the flow of contemplative life is interwoven with the rhythm of talking drums and bustling cities, rites of passage, and a communal witness to the difficulties of postcolonial life. From childbirth to death, spirit and flesh breathe as one; silences and ecstatic performance erupt during ritual and daily routines. Always the practices point beyond the visible to the invisible. Life is received as a gift and passed on as a legacy.

> Life is *one*. It is handed down from parents to children. . . .
> People know where their lives come from and that they are
> part of a stream of life that has always flowed through their
> family. The individual is nothing but the recipient of life,
> and has the duty to pass it on. What is important is not the
> individual, but the collective—the family, the clan, the
> whole people.[1]

Connections to spirits, holy and ancestral, are taken-for-granted aspects of indigenous African life. These ancestors are caretakers and guardians. Guardians are necessary because sometimes spirits make themselves known as trickster provocateurs. Sometimes during shamanic rituals bodily possession becomes the proof positive that reality is layered in the most incongruous of ways.

Because these journeys were saved for posterity in the memories of griots and drummers, objective linkages are tenuous at best. But I am not assuming that there will be retentions that are directly linked to Africa; instead I am seeking the cosmological orientations that contributed to contemplative undercurrents in Africana diasporan worship practices. This is neither theological tourism nor the quest for titillating exoticism. The hermeneutical lens that I am using to view African spiritual practices reveals the exotic stranger not just in indigenous cultures but also in the inner recesses of every human heart. On this planet, we are all indigenous strangers; some of us just have the good sense to know and embrace this reality.

Africa: The Land of Spiritual Origins

The most ironic turn of events in the twenty-first century is the discovery that all human beings are Africans. Archaeologists tell us that we are all the children of an African "Eve," the first human female. As a consequence, Africa's legacies belong not just to its people on the continent and in the diaspora but also to the global community. But exactly what is that legacy? Unfortunately, we have learned from the imperialists who invaded and divided the continent that Africa's contributions to the world community are limited to the tangible riches of the earth, that is, gold, diamonds, and fertile land.

Nevertheless, there are other riches ensconced in diverse contemplative religious traditions. These traditions focus attention on the spirit realm, daily communal flourishing, and an embodied spirituality deeply rooted in African culture. Although Africa's spiritual legacy includes its encounter with Christian, Jewish, and Muslim traditions, there were and still are indigenous contemplative religious expressions, which were firmly established before the monotheisms swept the continent.

Robert Williams notes that "the universe of African reality includes powers and principalities, ancestors and the cosmos."[2] Those who live in the midst of these realities recognize the fact that they are sharing an animate life world that is fully imbued with energy. Unlike western life spaces, which are crammed with purportedly lifeless and objective "tools" for human use and abuse, many African perspectives include the belief that everything has life and spiritual interiority. Although this view was deemed by outsiders to be infantile and animistic, it has been proven to have a closer affinity to the description of reality offered by theoretical physics than the west's studied abstractions. From this vibrant life view comes a contemplative perspective that is deeply relational and ecological.

Historical and Spiritual Resonances

Indigenous Cosmologies

Albert Raboteau refers to the African cosmos as a reality infused with historical and spiritual resonances. He believes that attention to the history of Christianity in its earliest stages reveals African origins deeply rooted in traditional practices. According to Raboteau, "ancient Christianity is not, as many think, a European religion. Christian communities were well established in Africa by the third and fourth centuries."[3] As a consequence, the contemplative practices that emerge in the diaspora have ties to Europe, the Middle East, and Africa.

As for spiritual resonances, Raboteau speaks of the superimposition of human and divine worlds. Each world is vibrant and populated with beings who can interact with one another through rituals and tradition. Ancestors have the ability to mediate and interfere, while gods, who represent varying character aspects of the high God, possess, visit, and guide. In his comparison of African indigenous practices with orthodoxy, Raboteau suggests that African spirituality invites the people to carry the power of God within them. This power is not limited to human vessels but can also be found in nature and in material objects.[4] "African spirituality does not dichotomize body and Spirit, but views the human being as embodied spirit and inspirited body, so that the whole person—body and spirit—is involved in the worship of God."[5] This means that a back flayed by a whip can become the conduit of worship, that the body hanging from a cypress tree plunges into the depths of God's own sorrow. In the midst of this theology is a presumption of metaphysical completion that is contemplative and extraordinary.

In African cosmologies contemplation is mystical, pragmatic, and efficacious. In fact, upon closer observation it becomes clear that contemplative spaces are ritual references to the silences from which we are born and into which we die. Our lives are bracketed by the liminal spaces that Victor Turner describes as betwixt and between realms of life and death. The African presumption is that we sojourn with God as God sojourns with us, and this mutual "abiding" takes place in a spiritually vigorous and responsive cosmos. African contemplations acknowledge spiritual entities and energies as part of the everyday world. One example of the manifestation of these energies can be found in the veneration of water spirits, that is, Mami Water (Wata).[6] This water spirit is represented by an element of nature, or a feminine or transgendered life force that mediates the confluence of human/divine interaction.[7] The water spirits beckon and teach devotees about the character of God and the wisdom of the ancestors.

Stories of the annual festival of Duola people provide a meaningful example of these interactive contemplative practices. It is said that once a year designated people enter the river to meet with the spirits and ancestors. They submerge without scuba gear or breathing equipment in full view of onlookers, beckoned by the water spirits. Dr. Marcel Oyono tells me that they dive to the bottom of the river and stay for hours at a time, returning with artifacts and gifts from the ancestors.[8] People speak of those encounters in ways that make it impossible to differentiate mythology and symbol from ascertainable action. In this instance, contemplation becomes a rhythm of life, a permeation of the ordinary with the surreal.

Robert Farris Thompson describes these ineffable moments within the context of Yoruban culture:[9] "The gods have 'inner' or 'spiritual' eyes . . . with which to see the world of heaven and 'outside eyes' . . . with which to view the world of men and women. When a person comes under the influence of a spirit . . . ordinary eyes swell to accommodate the inner eyes, the eyes of the god."[10] Farris describes the contemplative moment as an expansion of human perception and a visitation of God's unblinking inner and outer eye. When God is present, we respond in body and in spirit. Sometimes the eye swells, other times the feet leap, but inevitably the heart journeys home. This expansion of perception may occur, in the midst of a frenzied ritual possession, or in dramatic enactments of an intense and symbiotic relationship to the earth and the community. Such alliances cannot be sustained on a superficial level but must be expressed in the trans-species language of dance and trance. Entry into a reality without sociopolitical, scientific, or rational boundaries is unsettling, but it affords us the space for introspection. This process of self-reflection in the presence of God is critical to our survival; in many ways it is the unveiling of the secret we keep from one another—that we are strangers to ourselves. In the sections that follow, I consider contemplative practices as a cosmological orientation in African, Sufi, and indigenous practices.

African Contemplative Cosmologies

Olu Taiwo connects African worship practices to the mysteries of cosmology. He writes,

> As we approach the end of the second millennium, Newton's linear, fixed perception of time appears to have reached its limits, and new models are being and have been constructed . . . regarding the structure of matter in timespace. Einstein's "relativity" and Neils Bohr's "quantum mechanics" are two such examples.[11]

I understand Taiwo to be locating African (Yoruban) contemplative religious practices at the intersection of indigenous aesthetics and theoretical physics. Quantum physics is very weird science indeed! It verifiably describes scientific phenomena such as space-time continuums, spooky action at a distance, multiple universes, and indeterminacy, but it cannot tell us why these things are true. It is ironic that physicists still struggle to explain outcomes that defy established scientific laws, and yet, as Charles Finch notes, "everywhere in Africa, there exist men and women who claim to be able to see into the future, divine invisible causes and effects, affect events at a distance, and communicate with other beings—human and nonhuman—through psychic means."[12] For those Christians who consider the word *psychic* to be problematic, I suggest that Finch's observations be considered as fluctuations in the cosmological convergence of science, spirit, and flesh.

As for aesthetics, Taiwo links the inward turn with the art of mask-making and the "return beat" of ritual drummers. He notes that the west values "antique" masks and will pay a premium for ancient examples. Yet "for African mask makers the object, the mask has a ritual life span and it is this ritual life span, not only the mask, that has value (socially and spiritually rather than financially)."[13] Understanding and relating to the "life" of the ritual object begins the contemplative turn.

To be certain, I am using the word *contemplative* in a very different context. Taiwo uses the word *bliss* in the same way that I have been using *contemplative*. For the Yoruba, bliss is not just personal joy but an "inner glow." It is the ignition point for the reunion of the human heart with divine spirit. This event is not something within the control of the supplicant but rather "it is an expression of our transformative libido. Bliss opens playful energies, it mushrooms creative possibilities."[14]

This is the crux of the issue: contemplation in many African communities presumes the transcendence of actual physical realities, yet like everything else in the culture it is grounded theologically and philosophically in soil, sun, life, and death. Contemplation is not attenuated; it emanates from a situated stance. For the African the cosmos is the place where a special "quality or sacred power influences everything. Through sacrifice, divination, or the intensity of the dance, the consciousness of a devotee can be so transformed that the boundary between the ordinary and the extraordinary worlds becomes blurred."[15] This means that any individual or community has access to transformation. Behind the scrim of the ordinary world is another with portals accessible through dance, song, drumming, dreaming, and divination. "Ritual expression through music, art and movement acting together can bridge the differences between dimensionality, phase and frequency, for the individual by inviting us to partake in the co-creation of gnomonic space-time within the context of community."[16] One has to wonder what it is like to observe the ordinary world roll up like a curtain in the midst of communal devotion. Perhaps this is why rituals are so intentional; it would be most inconvenient if these dramatic transitions took place while gardens were being tended and food was being cooked.

Instead, the powers and principalities are recognized in everyday activity but are specifically invoked during designated rites. It is through the mediation of life's mysteries, through the pulsing beat of talking drums and the secrecy of initiation rites, that the community recognizes the unresolved dialectical tension between the seen and unseen worlds. Taiwo goes so far as to suggest that we are virtual beings, able to project our expectations and desires well beyond our four-dimensional reach through the art of storytelling and ritual reenactment. It is through rituals that we traverse the limits of time and space.

Contemplative Islam: Sufi Spirituality in Africa

"In forgetting God we have forgotten ourselves. Remembering God is the beginning of remembering ourselves."[17] Islamic contemplative traditions are important to this discussion because many Africans enslaved in the Americas were Muslim. Some scholars estimate that approximately forty thousand Muslims were transported to the Americas during slavery.[18] As a result Islamic approaches to the contemplative also contribute to the spiritual inclinations of the historical black church. Although there are many contemplative aspects of Islamic worship, I am briefly focusing on Sufism because it orients itself toward the mystical Spirit of God through devotional practices that subjugate the carnal to the spiritual.

The word *sufi* is said to be either Persian for the word *pure* or Arabic for the word *wool*. Historically adherents were known for their simple wool garments.[19] Sufism traces its origins to the prophet Muhammad and subsequent spiritual leaders, including the prophet's son-in-law Hazrati Ali.[20] Today the most well-known Sufi in the west is Mowlana Jalaluddin Rumi, a mystic poet often referred to by westerners simply as "Rumi." Sufis believe that "we arise from God and return to God," and this truth can be experienced and "known."[21] Rumi went further to attest to his belief that "all joy and all delight are found in God, and that God is to be found at this moment in the heart."[22] Rumi urges us to remain alert so that we do not miss the open portal into contemplative experiences. In fact, in the midst of oppression, remaining awake becomes a powerful resistance tool and a precursor to contemplation.

North Africa is one of the areas of concentrated Sufi practice. Other areas include Iran, Iraq, and Central Asia. Sufism became prevalent among African intellectuals in the eighteenth century in sub-Saharan Africa and later was an important influence across class divides.[23] Although Sufi scholars recognize the role that theological discourse plays in the interrogation of exterior and interior manifestations of the sacred, they prefer God's ongoing revelation through experience.

As a reform movement Sufism sought a "return to the purity and spirituality of Islam as it was in the time of the Prophet."[24] The intent was to transform human interiority through disciplined contemplative practices and movements. Sufis practice "a spiritual discipline intended to liberate the human spirit from its corporeal shell and enable it to move closer to God." They believe that this natural movement is hindered by the *nafs* or carnal soul.[25] The *nafs* is described as "malleable and changeable, responding to all kinds of social and personal stimuli. . . . By contrast, the spirit is stable and unchanging, reflecting its transcendent, divine origin."[26] Although Sufis engage in ritual practices to facilitate this flow toward God, they firmly believe that this union is a gift.

But how was this gift received by indigenous African communities? According to Louis Brenner there seem to be significant similarities between Sufism and African indigenous spiritual practices. Both acknowledge and interact with seen and unseen worlds; both believe that order in the seen world is directly linked to order in the invisible realm. Accordingly, both indigenous and Sufi community members strive to transcend the natural as a means of connection to ancestors and God. This goal is accomplished through the ritual guidance of specialized religious intermediaries and through initiation processes that transform the individual in ways that heighten awareness of the sacred.[27]

In Africa, Sufism emphasizes right relationships with nature, the living, and the dead. It presumes that the spiritual practices "transform an individual by imbuing him or her with new powers which give direct access to the hidden world. Such persons can 'see' what others cannot see."[28] Once again we are talking about the eye that "swells" so that divine insight can prevail. One religious cleric gives this testimony of calling and special sight:

> When I reached thirty-six years of age, God removed the veil from my sight, and the dullness from my hearing and my smell, and the thickness from my taste, and the cramp from my two hands, and the restraint from my two feet, and the heaviness from my body. . . . Then I found written upon my fifth rib, on the right side by the pen of Power, "Praise be to God, Lord of the Created Worlds" ten times . . . and I marvelled greatly at that.[29]

Clearly, these religious experiences confirm the Qur'an and the tenets of Islam. They also draw the devotee toward contemplation and provide an accessible platform for indigenous inculturation.

Indigenous Contemplative Perspectives: Initiation

The political correctness of recent years has left us with a plethora of unusable words. I am grateful that terms such as *primitive* and *pre-literate* are no longer acceptable descriptions of indigenous cultures. Graham Harvey, in his introduction to *Indigenous Religions*, notes the problematic aspect of words and descriptions used to preserve imperialistic presumptions about people and their cultures. This is particularly true since "indigenous religions are the majority of the world's religions."[30] Yet this label, "indigenous," tells us very little. It includes syncretic worship practices, an orientation toward spiritual energy and presence, and myriad other religious expressions.

In this section, I focus on three African indigenous contexts for contemplation, including rites of passage (birth and death), ritual drumming, and dance. We begin with initiation.

> Initiation into adulthood in black Africa represents precisely the contest between life and death and, in the end, the triumph of life. Initiation is not only a decisive experience bringing about a new state of being, a mode of existence in the world with reference to the ancestors; it is also a true language in itself.[31]

However, for the west, this language has often been unintelligible. Jean-Marc Ela wrests initiation from the imaginations of western imitators to explicate this intense cultural experience through the lens of African belief systems. Rites of passage as identified by Arnold van Gennep are "the transitional rituals accompanying changes of place, state, social position and age in a culture."[32] They demarcate life stages and teach young men and women the secrets of adulthood. They also empower initiates by testing the courage and resolve of those who will lead the community into the future.

Each community has its own purposes and goals for initiation. But beyond the practical need to prepare the next generation for their moral obligations, initiations reinforce the communal cosmology. "The goal of the secret societies is to learn to master forces of the visible and invisible realms for the benefit of the community."[33] This aspect of initiation occurs outside of the confines of the village but benefits all. A Yoruban priest explains the experience in this way:

> All people who go to the sacred bush [igbodu] benefit from it; they may be observers; they may be priests; they may be the initiate. . . . We are reborning ourselves. Even we priests, we are getting another rebirth. At every ritual, we are becoming new because we have something to reflect upon. We have something to contemplate during the journey, at the journey, after the journey. Our brains become sharper. We become new to the world. We think of everything. We *do* there, and we *see* there. And even more simply we pray for every body.[34]

Initiates are secluded in ways that induce the contemplative journey. Although they are with peers, the fear of the unknown, the isolation from family and the community, the tasks and sojourn with ancestors all serve to disconnect them from the everyday world. Ela equates this time in the bush to a symbolic death of youth and the emergence of the adult.[35] The initiates are in a focused spiritual environment that forces them to view their past and future from a completely different perspective. Initiates become open vessels receiving the wisdom of the elders; more important, they take their places on the great wheel of life that turns elders into ancestors and children into adults. They learn to embrace the spirit realm and to understand that life is never linear but a cycle of spiritual seasons. Ela says it best when he describes initiation as a reenactment of the genesis of the universe, an embodied realization that everything old is new again.[36]

With this knowledge, suffering will not be the crucible that breaks their spirits, loss will be assuaged by the potential for rebirth, and the host of elements in nature and the spirit realm will guide and taunt in ways that hone their humanity. This is not contemplation as defined by monastics throughout the ages, but it is a centered and reflective experience that unifies body and spirit, enlightens the soul, and prepares the initiate for the constant interplay between mystery and everyday survival.

Contemplating Beginnings and Endings: Indigenous Perspectives

Birth

In African societies each life is an occasion that celebrates the return of an ancestor in the newborn child. The child's potential, ancestral linkages, and spirit are discerned through rites centered on a contemplative analysis of the umbilical cord and placenta and a communal call to the child who is journeying between worlds. Birthing celebrates new life, but the newness is old, for every child is an old soul seeking reunion with the community.

The birth rituals of the Yoruba (in Nigeria) provide meaningful examples of West African contemplative practices. In a traditional Yoruban community, birthing takes place at home with the help of older women, unless an emergency necessitates medical intervention. "At the final stages of labor, the woman goes on her knees. It is in that position she delivers her baby. It is a most memorable day in the life of a mother. It is called *Ojo Ikunle Abiyamo* (the day of the kneeling mother)."[37] In this supplicated position Yoruban mothers become physical conduits between worlds.

Malidome Somé describes the birth rituals of the Dagara people, located in Burkina Faso, West Africa. The Dagaran birth ritual includes the walking of the mother during labor. The women chant to her as she walks, addressing the soon-to-arrive child. The chants coax and entreat the child to enter the world. They chant softly, "you have come to a crossroads. The light you see in front of you is the light of the village that awaits you," or they may say, "run, run, run to the gate and do not waste time, because Mummy is in pain."[38] The singing continues until the moment of birth. Then the women and children gather for the serious work of delivery. Somé tells us that the children of the village are present and are expected to cry out in answer to the first cry of the newborn. The cry of the children "satisfies something in the psy-che of the [newborn], who is now ready to surrender to being present in this world."³⁹ Somé's stunning observation is that when the children cry out in answer to the newborn, they are offering assurances that this child will not journey in the world alone. He wonders about western birthing rituals that allow newborns to wail without an answering cry. He asks, "Can infants recover from the damage done to their souls as a result of a mes-sage at birth that they are on their own?"⁴⁰

After the birth, the naming ceremonies begin. There are three categories: names that reflect parental expectations; names given at the moment of birth that reflect unusual occurrences related to the birth, unique physical attributes of the child, or an analysis of the position of the umbilical cord.⁴¹ In traditional communi-ties the first few days of birth draw the mother and child into a close circle of ritual seclusion in preparation for reentry into soci-ety. The rituals vary according to tribes but emphasize purifica-tion, a period of focused bonding, and the intentional separation of the child from the spirit realm.

John Mbiti discusses the prohibitions that protect the preg-nant mother and unborn child; for example, a commonsense rule forbids eating meat killed with poisoned arrows. But there are also rules that speak to an intuitive understanding of the need for emotional health. Mao couples must communicate through an intermediary, forestalling the discord that may occur during a pregnancy, thereby protecting the mother from distress.⁴² These prohibitions address issues of maternal/child care and the spiri-tual well-being of both. The actual birth of a baby is of interest to the entire community because everyone wants to know who is coming back from the spirit realm, who is emerging from the silence.

Today there are few traditional communities that adhere com-pletely to these cultural practices. However the African history of contemplative naming and birthing is consonant with a world-view that prioritizes wisdom from every spectrum of the life space. One journeys into and out of life in the midst of a con-cerned community.

Death

"Death in Afro cultures is generally not something to be feared, but a transitory rupture to be greeted. If it is a 'good death,' it evinces a return and reunion with the dead and the ancestors."[43] In West African culture, death is also an entry point, an event that is surrounded by the ceremonies and contemplative preparation of the community. Although the event is disruptive to community life, there are methods for resolving the final mystery. Death is one of the rhythms of life; it is the portal that leads to the spirit world. Mbiti describes the removal of a dead relative through a hole in the residence rather than the door—a tangible sign that this is a transition and not a final departure.[44] Although deaths are often attributed to sorcery or other malevolent forces, the community can reclaim the moment through its care of the dying. African culture recognizes stages of being beyond physical embodiment. Upon death the person moves into the living-dead stage and eventually (depending on the circumstances of death) may transition to ancestor status.

Robert Hood reminds us that in traditional African cultures, great care is taken to assuage the spirits of the dead through elaborate burial rites, dinners, and remembrance dates. Birth and death are inextricably linked. Traditionalist Zulus of South Africa bury their death in a fetal position to mimic the position of a fetus in the womb. Moreover, "the place of burial is called the navel, indicating hope in rebirth or being 'born again' into the family through reincarnation."[45] Others dress their dead in elaborate costumes and seat them in a place of honor as ceremonies proceed. Yoruban traditions include seven days of ritual mourning, feasting, and public ritual performance. The deceased is ritually washed, as is the coffin. Kolawole Ositala describes communal acts of wrapping the body in cloth. Finally, the deceased is feted at a party in preparation for transition to the ancestors. "After the lid of the coffin is closed, the eldest child takes the . . . brass staff and raps it three times near the corpse's head. The knocking dispatches the soul of the deceased."[46]

During death rituals in traditional communities, the community participates in the suspension of ordinary time. Unusual events are expected as the community accompanies the deceased toward the spirit realm. Grieving and celebration share space during the period of bereavement and communal readjustment. Whether in birth or death, life is a journey. Part of the journey is on well-worn life paths traversed by ancestors; other roads must be carved out of impossibility.

Indigenous Rhythms: Drums, Music, and Dance

"Bible, Qur'an, and Drum have the same vocation; these are fundamental sacred 'books' venerated by their respective peoples. They are monuments of the human spirit because they are timeless."[47] The drum is a timeless instrument. It acts as a conduit that draws the listener toward the sacred realm within and without. In the drum rhythms ancestors hear and remember their responsibilities to the living; the living hear the beating heart of an ongoing universe and reorder their priorities so that their life energy is attuned to the pulse of life. This intuitive tuning occurs in cultures around the planet. It occurs as infants in their mother's womb align their sense of well-being with their mother's heartbeat. It occurs inexplicably when the menstrual cycles of women synchronize while they are collaborating on a creative project or living in close proximity to one another.

In West Africa the contemplative heritage was etched into the souls of adherents through rhythmic, percussive, ritualistic, and musical enactments. There are rhythms in our finely tuned cosmos that have been overwhelmed by the hum of technology and the constant noise of postmodernity. And yet there are still a few places in the world where those rhythms are apparent and necessary to the flourishing of human life. As certainly as the waves of the sea induce a sense of reunion with nature, so also are the drums of Africa linked to contemplative practices. The drum is a percussive instrument that infuses a rhythmic ontology into all spectrums of a multivalent life space.

The talking drum is a very special drum that is not just a percussive instrument but also a keeper of cultural history and an
important part of community life. Georges Niangoran-Bouah
describes the character of the talking drum as an instrument with
animation, orality, memory, and language: "as a living being, a
drum can speak."[48] It sends and receives inquiries from the
ancestors, and it reminds villagers that those who have died
recently are traversing the rivers on their journey to the spirit
realm.

When Niangoran-Bouah says that the drum is an "animated
being" imbued with spiritual force and vitality, he refers to a life
force evoked and manifested in the drum.[49] In Akan culture, the
drum is believed to be a gift from the creator. The drum is guest
and griot at ceremonies and is afforded respect that is similar to
the deference afforded the Christian communion cup and plates.
Respect for the ritual elements of communion is the natural consequence of the belief that they are either symbolically or actually in contact with the body and blood of Jesus.

In similar fashion, talking drums in Akan culture are in contact
with the creator and can mediate between realms. In other West
African communities the gods inhabit the drum and speak to the
drummers and listeners through the rhythms.[50] Niangoran-
Bouah completes his analysis of the talking drum by describing it
as a repository of the history of a people, its memory, and its language. He argues that "the texts of a talking drum are as reliable
as those of the written word."[51] In fact the drum itself offers a
language that is as meaningful and complex as human speech. It
is the instrument of celebration, seeking, and inspiration, an
accompaniment to contemplation and ritual.

Musicologist W. Komla Amoaku is a member of the Ewe tribe
of Ghana. He shares the contemplative transitions that occur
when he plays the music of his culture:

> I can define traditional African music only from within the
> Ewe world view. For me, it is the involuntary alteration that
> occurs in my psyche, the spiritual upliftment, my transcen-
> dental imaginations of a spirit world, my oneness with the

gods and spirits of departed relatives, and that temporary transformation of my physical body into spirit. Whenever I participate in this music, whether physically or silently, I look for the properties that make the activity spiritually satisfying and fulfilling—properties that link me with the invisible world and constantly remind me of a world beyond.[52]

Amoaku is careful to assess the music of Africa within its own cultural framework. Amoaku describes an alteration in everyday reality structures. To be more precise, he has an awakening to the connections of the universe that are usually hidden under the matrix of false assumptions of separation and radical individualism.

Whether these transitions between everyday life and the spirit realm are actual, psychological, or beyond our comprehension has not yet been settled. However, there have been studies that link alpha brainwave states to drumming. The alpha state refers to a dream-like detachment and physical relaxation. The pattern of drumbeats seems to calm and focus the mind. "When the mind fixates . . . a profound state of Silence ensues."[53] Silence is an odd word to use in the midst of the cacophony of many drums. Yet the stillness referenced is akin to the intense spiritual engagement that marks the contemplative experience. Different drum rhythms evoke different spirits, and contemplative movements are active, reciprocal, and communal.

The community seeks divine presence together and mediates the power of those moments when God dwells with them through collective ritual events led by designated spiritual leaders. These leaders have power by virtue of a spiritual calling, because of birthright (they are deemed to bear the spirit of an ancestor priest or powerful spiritual mediator), or because they have visions indicating selection by ancestral spirits.

Africans traditionalists tend to be highly suspicious of those who evoke spiritual powers without the express designation of the community or their oversight. Although some of the "witch hunting" that still occurs is a function of bias related to gender, class, or diminished social status, some fears become malevolent expressions of communal scapegoating when individuals approach or appropriate spiritual power without the blessing and participation of the community. Anything that cannot be done in the presence of the community is problematic.

Dancing with Mystery

"Africans and African Diasporans and our spiritual beings have defined music and dance as a profound style of expression of the divine essential to the functioning of the universe, representing the most fundamental principles of the cosmic system, and a privileged form of communication between humans and the divine."[54] A path leads into the heart of contemplation, but there is no signage to guide the way. One finds that one has arrived without realizing one has embarked. Portals open as the quickening steps of seekers engage a dancing God in a dancing universe. If there is any way to dialogue with the God who created a universe of vibrating and dancing "strings," perhaps it is through dance.

Kofi Agawu says that "rhythm refers to a binding together of different dimensional processes, a joining rather than a separating, an across-the dimensions instead of within-the dimension phenomenon."[55] At the very least there is an embodied knowing that exceeds the limits of rational thought.[56] During dance the body is submitted for possession and symbolic display but also for a dance with mystery that indistinguishably weds dance to contemplation and trance. Yet these connections are within the control of the community and express their moods and intent.

Daphne Harrison describes dance-songs that range from competitive, communal, and ecstatic performance to possession and parody.[57] One thing is certain: in a social context that is permeated with life of all sorts, people need the community to interpret, intercede, and ameliorate not only possession rituals but also social and psychic dysfunction. These movements are contemplative because they enact the inward journey in external ways. Those engaged in these ritual acts address issues of concern in the community through gestures and facial expressions. Enemies might be brought together to shake hands; couples in conflict might be pressed into an involuntary embrace. In this context the rituals of contemplation are shared and public. Dance, drumming, and initiation rites offer one of the preeminent opportunities for the community to engage in the joint process of social functioning and spiritual mediation.

However, these activities only point to the general location of contemplative experiences. There is always more happening than can be witnessed by observers. In this discussion, I want to mention one last contemplative element found in West African spiritual life. In Yoruban culture there is a contemplative rhythm that is not articulated in dance or drumming. Taiwo names the experience the "return beat," and describes it as "an ontological experience of the tempo . . . the spaces between the beats." According to Taiwo, these silent rhythms emerge from a "non-linear dimension" like waves of energy with the power to repel and attract.[58]

Return beats are the spaces between breaths, syncopated by the silent rhythm of the heart and the ever-so-slight pause between thoughts. In every circumstance there is a pronounced rhythm of life and an undercurrent, a return beat that attracts the contemplative listener. Whether we are on the continent or in the diaspora, when we live into the return beat, "we can then understand the subtle para-linguistic, non-verbal codes . . . rooted in the body."[59] Contemplation that arises from music, ritual passages, demonstrative movement, and the listening for return beats offers a rich resource for our renewal.

What Is Africa to Me?[60]

I began this chapter with the phrase "Africa, my Africa" and end it with the question that the poet Countee Cullen posed: What is Africa to me? My answer to this question is that Africa is a wellspring of contemplative practices—spiritual quests that benefit the community as well as the individual. From drums and dance to the spinning contemplative movements of the Sufis, embodied indigenous responses to the sacred are integral to spiritual reflection. These contemplative practices emerge from the realization that God's presence cannot be contained in one song, prayer, or religious ritual. Rather, myriad responses are necessary to grasp the ineffable. But these responses must be linked by the expectations and commitment of the community.

The power of restoration requires the amalgam of intention and destiny. The continent of Africa today is devastated by AIDS and the residual effects of decades of colonization and exploitation. The diasporan communities in the Americas and around the globe lie devastated by nihilism, isolation, and the lure of consumer satisfactions. We have gone so far down different paths that one wonders whether the spiritual reunion of Africa's scattered progeny is possible. If there are to be spiritual returns, they will begin with a reclamation of the African journey inward—a ritual space for the embrace of the sold, stolen, and colonized.

3
Every Shut Eye Ain't Sleep
The Inner Life during Slavery

We come through the dead: forgetfulness of their struggles
dehumanizes us and cultivates a callousness toward time and
the possibilities it affords us.
　　—Josiah Ulysses Young III

We can cry over loss, but not as if the loss is everything.
　　—Victor Anderson

Whatever African retentions are found in black worship did not
get there by a direct route, but were transmuted and filtered by
the Middle Passage's incommunicability. Meaning had to be
uttered rather than spoken through something more primal
than the particularity of language—the moan.
　　—James A. Noel

The air must have been thick with fear and prayer as the slaving
ships pulled out of Goree and other West African ports laden
with human cargo. Devotees of Vodun, the river gods, Yahweh,
Allah, Olodumare—to name just a few—lay together (tightly or
loosely packed) in an involuntary rebirthing cocoon. It was a
community of sorts, yet each person lay in their own chrysalis of
human waste and anxiety. More often than not, these Africans
were strangers to each other by virtue of language, culture, and
tribe. Although the names of their deities differed, they shared a
common belief in the seen and unseen. The journey was a rite of
passage of sorts that stripped captives of their personal control

over the situation and forced them to turn to the spirit realm for relief and guidance.

In this chapter I explore communal contemplation in the midst of terror, as Africans arrived in the Americas. Once again the word *contemplation* must press beyond the constraints of religious expectations to reach the potential for spiritual centering in the midst of danger. Centering moments accessed in safety are an expected luxury in our era. During slavery, however, crisis contemplation becomes a refuge, a wellspring of discernment in a suddenly disordered life space, and a geospiritual anvil for forging a new identity. This definition of contemplation is dynamic and situational. Accordingly I will focus on three exemplary situations that evoke the contemplative.

The first contemplative opportunity occurs during the Middle Passage in the holds of slave ships, the second can be identified on the auction blocks, and the third emerges in the hush arbors. Each event is experienced by individuals stunned into multiple realities by shock, journey, and displacement. As unlikely as it may seem, the contemplative moment can be found at the very center of such ontological crises. In the words of Howard Thurman, "when all hope for release in this world seems unrealistic and groundless, the heart turns to a way of escape beyond the present order."[1] For captured Africans there was no safety except in common cause and the development of internal and spiritual fortitude.

Crossing the "Bitter Waters"

Lamine Kebe uses the phrase *bitter waters* to describe not just the ocean but also the trauma of the transatlantic passages of Africans into the Americas.[2] Although the event is often referred to as the Middle Passage, this label fails to depict the stark realities of a slave ship. Captured Africans were spooned together lying on their sides in ships that pitched with every wave. Together they wept and moaned in a forced community that cut across tribal and cultural lines. They were a people who had not been a people, even though they shared similar cosmologies. On the continent they revered ancestors who were born and reborn into the lives of future generations. Spirits, good and bad, permeated the everyday world and opened the vistas of the natural world in ways that sensitized them to the life energy in the entire universe. These life forces were necessary for daily sustenance and spiritual well-being. They also helped to maintain the delicate balances of life in agrarian communities. For centuries the balances had been maintained. Now each chained African wondered whether he or she had fallen through the spiritual safety net provided by spirits and ancestors into the stifling ship's hold.

In his book *Terror and Triumph* Anthony Pinn discusses the Middle Passage as the horrific transition from personhood to property and non-identity. The journey can be characterized as "rupture." Using powerful birth metaphors, Pinn quotes Michael Gomez, who writes, "the African died to what was and to what could have been."[3] Pinn concludes that the journey was crucial to the formation of a slave. Black people left as Africans connected to continent, ancestors, and the local community; they were reborn as property. This is a ritual passage, a rebirth from one reality to another.[4]

Arnold van Gennep identified the three phases of ritual passage as separation, margin or limen, and reaggregation.[5] The separation from context was actual and psychic for Africans during the Middle Passage. Chained in the hold, they entered the liminal phase of ritual passage described as "betwixt and between."[6] I find this term and Victor Turner's subsequent description of this altered reality instructive and uncanny in their similarity to the plight of enslaved Africans. During this stage "liminars are stripped of status and authority, removed from a social structure maintained and sanctioned by power and force, and leveled to a homogeneous social state through discipline and ordeal. Their secular powerlessness may be compensated for by a sacred power."[7] The power that Turner describes as sacred has a horizon of meaning that includes human resilience and divine omniscience. Divine and profane responses to suffering are not mutually exclusive. They intersect with one another in ways that confound our ability to attribute survival to one cause or another. Slavery does not represent ordinary suffering. It is one of many unique situations that far exceed the limits of human imagination and assessment. Holocausts against one group or another cannot be contained within the bounds of the individual human body. Instead, oppression of this magnitude forces a community beyond courage and individual survival skills into a state of unresolved shock and disassociation. Under these conditions, the interiority of the community becomes a living "flow" that sustains the afflicted. But this flow also pulls the weak toward death, even as it insures the survival of the community.

Mihaly Csikszentmihalyi's term *flow* seems to apply in this situation. Even though its original usage applies to play, sports, and enjoyment, the definition also encompasses religious ritual. Flow is described as "the merging of action and awareness"[8] and as a generative life-sustaining energy that moves individuals toward unity. He says that "flow is made possible by a centering of attention on a limited stimulus field, by means of bracketing, framing, and often a set of rules. There is a loss of ego, and the self becomes irrelevant."[9] This flow may have been the impetus that allowed crisis contemplation to emerge.

Why Have You Forsaken Me?

The hold of the slave ship becomes the stage upon which the human drama unfolds. Here the field of reference is excruciatingly limited. Although unity is the ultimate outcome of flow, angst and anguish are the fertile sites of its emergence. Strangers linked by destiny and chains focused their intentions on survival instead of the unrelenting pain, because pain that does not abate cannot be integrated into human reality structures.

I am reminded of the stark description that William Stringfellow uses with regard to his own pain: "Pain is not a punishment; neither is pain a justification. There are no grounds to be romantic about pain; pain is a true mystery, so long as this world lasts. Yet it is known that pain is an intercessory: one is never alone in pain but is always a surrogate of everyone else who hurts—which is categorically everybody."[10] No matter how personal the pain may seem, Stringfellow recognizes the universal nature of suffering. It is a human state that we are reluctant to examine closely. It is far easier to handle mass pain as a distant anomaly, familiar and dismissable. Even when the sounds and sights of human despair seem familiar, ultimately we must admit that we were mistaken. The human mind cannot know the entire meaning of another person's pain.

Ultimately, our objective tools for analyzing and interpreting pain will always fail us, because there is an aspect of suffering that is not within our rational reach. Pain is a parallel universe that sends shockwaves breaking over our consciousness, daring us to succumb. The only hope of understanding it comes as we align ourselves with a groaning universe committed to cycles of birth, rebirth, and the longing for a just order. As Eric Cassell puts it, "suffering arises with the 'loss of the ability to pursue purpose.' Thus in suffering we face the loss of our own personal universe. In order to claim some hold on that universe, the suffering need to articulate the fears, hopes and concerns that they have."[11] Elaine Scarry does not agree with Cassell's call for articulation.[12] To the contrary, Scarry contends that torturers are empowered by the cries of the tortured, because the voice betrays the body in its affirmation of the torturer's purported power.[13] I think that each situation requires a different response. But sometimes words will not come either to affirm or to betray. It is at that time that the moan becomes the vehicle for articulating that which can never be voiced.

Moans are the utterances of choice when circumstances snatch words and prayers from bereft lips. As time went on, the moans from the slave ship's cargo hold lost their human sound, for there is no bodily response that could assuage or comfort, no sound that could fully express the horror. If there were such a sound or expression adequate for the task, it would break the hearts of all who heard it.

Moaning over the Bitter Waters

The moan became the first vocalization of a new spiritual vocabulary—terrible and wonderful, it was a cry, a critique, a prayer, a hymn, a sermon, all at once. . . . The moan expressed loneliness, pain, and the inchoate hope which would later fuse with biblical imagery. Its rhythm was not so much the syncopated beat of the West African drum as the rock and sway of the sea-faring vessel which contained their bodies.[14]

The only sound that would carry Africans over the bitter waters was the moan. Moans flowed through each wracked body and drew each soul toward the center of contemplation. As I noted at the beginning of this chapter, the word *contemplation* seems inappropriate for this context. Contemplation usually occurs at the leisure of one who has the freedom to decide how to enter into the divine presence. It is purportedly the epitome of peace and repose. However, contemplation can also be a displacement of the ordinary, a paradigm shift that becomes a temporary refuge when human suffering reaches the extent of spiritual and psychic dissolution. It can be a state of extraordinary spiritual attenuation, a removal to a level of reality that allows distance from excruciating circumstances.

The portal to this reality can best be described as a break in the ordinary, exposing the complexity and chaos of a universe that sanctions both pleasure and pain. If the journey is as liminal as it is actual, the moan is the vehicle that carries the afflicted community toward transcendence. James Noel notes that the moan articulates the sighs and groans of the spirit. It is the very essence of protest and prayer, a "spirit song," as it were, in rhythmic sway with the lurching of slave ships and terrorized souls.[15] It is a sound that rides the crest of communal longing and angst. As Noel correctly suggests, no other sound could adequately express the "incommunicability" of the Middle Passage.[16]

In support of Noel's statement, we have the testimony of Olaudah Equiano (1745–1797), a slave born in Benin. His narrative offers a concrete example of the context for the moan as the beginning of Africana crisis contemplation. Upon being captured by slavers, he describes an anguish too profound for words:

> The only comfort we had was in being in one another's arms [he refers to his sister] that night and bathing each other with our tears. But alas! We soon despaired of even the small comfort of weeping together. The next day . . . she was torn from me. . . . I was left in a state of distraction not to be described. I cried and grieved continually; and for several days did not eat anything but what they forced into my mouth.[17]

On the transatlantic journey, Equiano says, "the shrieks of the women and the groans of the dying rendered the whole a scene of horror almost inconceivable."[18] There were no words adequate enough to express the sorrow chained in the hold of slaver ships, and so the moan billows out of the stench and begins its ascent toward the heavens.

Most of the captured Africans were in shock. The shift from participation in a highly articulate African culture to confinement in cargo ships was stunning in its abruptness. Yet West Africans brought with them unique cultural resources gleaned from communal life. They were familiar with innovation and embodied narrative. On the continent, life was dialogical but not confined to the contestations of the human voice. That which could not be spoken was danced, drummed, or resolved ritually. But this event was different. There was no experiential or spiritual reference point for the Middle Passage, no linguistic counterpart. Articulation of such events cannot be contained by ordinary language processes; rather, human responses must unfold with the experience. In the ships' holds, words were replaced with whispered prayers and nonverbal utterances that pointed to the place where language or silence should be.

I began this book with a description of the moan contextualized within an African American worship service. So much meaning was ensconced in the words "oh, oh, oh, Jesus." The moan as it emerges during the Middle Passage is also a genera-

tive sound. One imagines the Spirit moaning as it hovered over
the deep during the Genesis account of creation. Here the moan
stitches horror and survival instincts into a creation narrative, a
tapestry of historical memory that marks the creation of community. On the slave ships the moan became the language of stolen
strangers, the articulation of unspeakable fears, the precursor to
joy yet unknown. The moan is the birthing sound, the first movement toward a creative response to oppression, the entry into the
heart of contemplation through the crucible of crisis.

Dancing on Deck

Lament was the discourse in the hold, as captives moaned their
prayers. On deck after evening rations, lament danced and
swayed under the watchful eyes of the crew. Robert Harms
reports that accordions often provided the incongruous music on
French slave ships.[19] There is no comparison between a talking
drum and an accordion to listeners familiar with one or the
other. So these dances could not have been exact reenactments
of familiar rituals on the continent. Instead, forced to dance or
sing, Africans expanded their musical vocabulary. They listened
to one another sing the songs of their villages and learned
through the differences of rhythm and movement that diversity
would be the foundation of their new community. It is likely that
these on-deck command performances took on an intensity and
intent to invoke the gods who had seemingly deserted them.

Olly Wilson interprets a well-known West African aphorism,
"The Gods will not descend without song,"[20] to mean that music
is critical to African cosmologies. It is also a reminder to the
devotees of African deities to implore their gods for relief. In the
midst of entreaty and forced movement, something new was
being born. The dances of their ancestors were now permeated
with laments that acted as a counterpoint to the forced jigs on
deck. Sterling Stuckey captures the intensity of dance memory
when he says that dance was the most difficult of all art forms to
erase from the slave's memory. The body that was subjected to

abuse also had a memory capable of "inscribing in space the language of the human spirit."[21]

Arriving on Distant Shores

When Africans arrived in the Americas, they were faced with the challenge of translating crisis communities formed in slavers' holds into viable and responsive systems of support. These communities could not be geographically limited; rather, they had to be loosely and spiritually bound by common purposes, so that those who were sold or escaping could reenter at any time or place. The fluidity of these communities maximized the potential for interaction with diverse religious beliefs and traditions. Muslim, indigenous, Jewish, and Christian adherents formed a creative synthesis that borrowed the most viable and portable aspects of their religious proclivities as the basis for communal worship.

Auction Laments:
Carrying a Flag and Ringing a Bell

As the system of breeding labor became the primary means of replenishing slave stock in the United States, the auction blocks became the second site of crisis contemplation. Auction blocks can be considered sacred communal spaces where familial bonds were shattered and pilgrimages began and ended. One could hear the sounds of the auctioneer interplay with the shrieks of children and the tears of the separated. Relationships were so transitory that one could not risk the casual negligence that characterizes many postmodern associations. One had to live into relationships fully because they were so fragile and transitory within the institutional framework of slavery.

The era of auction blocks has slipped away so that we have no sense of what the experience was like or how the block became the locus of inward journeys. Horation J. Eden, who was enslaved as a child in Kentucky and Tennessee, wrote:

I was born in Memphis, my master being Dr. Hall. When he decided to sell me and my mother, he sent us to the Negro yard—a camp to be sold. It was in Memphis—I do not know where. I was young but I remember well some things I saw there. The yard . . . [was] a kind of square stockade of high boards with two room negro houses around, say three sides of it & high board fence too high to be scaled. . . . We were all kept in these rooms, but when an auction was held or buyers came we were brought out and paraded two or three around a circular brick walk in the center of the stockade. The buyers would stand near by and inspect us as we went by, stop us and examine us. Our teeth, & limbs and a Doctor generally if there were sick negroes.[22]

The circular movement around the "yard" is familiar in contemplative history. From the labyrinth to the ring shout people have attached theological significance to circular movements. Most of the walking rituals are positive. They signify the release of human burdens within the unity of the circle, the centering of spirit and soul, and a symbol of incarnated and embodied potential. The circular movement described in this slave narrative is a wicked unwinding of personal integrity and sanity. It evokes the same crisis response that occurred in the hold of slave ships.

Essentially, the auction block becomes a vortex of negative spiritual intention that draws all participants willing or not into its reality structure. This means that even the slave traders were knit into this space. To contextualize this idea, Dwight Hopkins describes the roles of whites at every class level with regard to the sale and transportation of enslaved Africans. The lower classes were relegated to patrollers, "nigger hunters," and slave whippers. At the middle-class level, whites were involved with the business aspect of slavery. They traded and owned Negro pens and auction blocks.[23] They also helped the system by capturing free slaves and offering them for sale. The slaves were not free, but neither were the people charged with the responsibility of enforcing oppression.

The 1840 account of a free man, Stephen Dickenson Jr., is especially poignant. He was employed as a ship fireman on the steamboat *New Castle*. After leaving the port of New York, the ship docked in New Orleans, where he was captured with his friends and enslaved. "We were delivered to the auctioneer by the name of Rudisill, who paraded us about the streets for about an hour offering us for sale, compelling one of us to carry a red flag, and another of us to ring a bell. But as no one offered a satisfactory price for us . . . we were put up at auction."[24] Dickenson describes a solemn sale procession. I have attended "high church" rituals where the services are preceded by a processional, incense, and liturgical flags. At those times, one can imagine all of the processionals that preceded us in the history of human faith. Processionals are used in preparation for wars, on behalf of God, as funereal recognition of a life that has slipped behind the veil. In the historical context of slave auctions, the procession becomes a somber bell-ringing march to display the merchandise of human bodies. This march was integral to the crisis contemplation that I have identified with the auction block and its catastrophic ruptures of life and spirit.

Here the slave traders forced enslaved Africans to be complicit in their own continued enslavement. "When a negro was put on the block he had to help sell himself by telling what he could do. If he refused to praise himself and acted sullen he was sure to be stripped and given thirty lashes. Frequently a man was compelled to exaggerate his accomplishments, and when his buyer found he could not do what he said, he would be beaten unmercifully. It was pretty sure to be a thrashing either way."[25]

It was not unusual to hear the lament of the entire community when a general sale was scheduled: "The cries and tears of brothers, sisters, wives and husbands were heard in the same streets; for on that day a general sale of slaves used to take place. But now he hoped that God would bury the slave auctioneer's voice in the dust, and that it should never be heard again."[26] This statement was made by William Davis, an enslaved African who was brought to a church meeting by a missionary society to talk about providing for the needs of local slaves. According to John

Blassingame, the story appeared in the *New York Times* on January 14, 1862. The Rev. L. S. Lockwood introduced Davis as "one of Uncle Sam's slaves." His plea for God's intervention to silence his enemy is reminiscent of the laments in the Psalms. Davis did not ask that the auctions stop or that God turn the forces of nature against the enemies of enslaved Africans; instead he asked that the voice be silenced. Davis knew that the power of life and death is in the tongue. If freedom is not on the horizon—and it did not seem that it was—then the least that God can do is silence the oppressors. Davis was advocating silence as respite from oppression. Although thoughtful silence and prayer should be entered voluntarily, crisis situations require crisis tactics. Under ordinary circumstances contemplative silences open the human spirit to new perspectives and divine order. When evil is the only matrix, silencing the voice of the oppressor is a first step toward justice and peace.

The auction blocks remind us of the horror of slavery. We have to wonder how those involved in the trade survived. This question encompasses not just the captive Africans but all involved in the maintenance of this malevolent system. Howard Thurman gives us a hint as to ways in which crisis contemplation helps to sustain people. He suggests alternatives, which include mercilessness and bitterness, withdrawal, or creativity exercised as "a great and dynamic will."[27] Thurman offers either/or options; I would suggest that the lines of demarcation are blurred, because a response to radical evil may contain in its potential enactment both creativity and bitterness. Moreover, the will to survive is saturated with perpetual lament. As Thurman so aptly puts it, "[S/]he goes on because [s/]he must go on."[28] It is the turn toward the contemplative that loosens the "psychological shackles." When people under siege face the power within, they uncover "a bottomless resourcefulness . . . that ultimately enables [the person] to transform the spear of frustration into a shaft of light."[29] As William Johnston notes, "the light is a gift. No one can arouse it by human effort."[30] The conversion stories confirm this "gift" as an imparted peace in the midst of bondage.

Plantation Practices:
Always Looking beyond the Blue

The last example of crisis contemplation occurred on the plantations. Here enslaved Africans created narratives of survival that depended on personal courage and God's deliverance. The word *courageous* within the context of slavery is problematic because it has incongruous but romantic overtones. Those who attempt to describe the horrors of one holocaust or another inevitably use language that romanticizes the oppression until it takes on mythic proportions. When history is collapsed into myth, responsibilities become diffused, and repentance and reconciliation become impossible.

In the inflated realm of mythical oppression, villains are so villainous that no one sees themselves reflected in the image. Few can trace accrued privileges to specific and intentional evil acts. Similarly, victims become so quintessentially and epically victimized that all escape routes from the condition are sealed off by a maze of self-doubt, blaming, and low self-esteem. The antidote to this phenomenon is to attend to the details, to understand the specific events, ancestors, life stories, causes of oppression, and avenues of social change. Historical and spiritual specificity is salvific. Then and only then can the movement toward moral flourishing begin.

Contemplating Radical Evil

The specificity that is called for begins with the inward glance, the personal accountability within a gathered community. Gathering this information is not as easy as it seems because of the continued secret-keeping and avoidance. I heard some of the stories as I grew up; others are known but not repeated. I have asked my mother, who is now eighty-six years old, why there seem to be so many secrets about the old days now that we are well into the twenty-first century. Her reply is one I have heard before from American Indians and Latin American refugees: it is too painful to talk about. She remembers that when the elders tried to tell some of the stories of oppression, silent tears would flow without ceasing. Some things, she says, must be forgotten in order to forgive. Although I do not argue this point with her, I am convinced that this type of communal response to suffering can become a cultural malignancy. In times past, intentional cultural amnesia may have proven to be an efficacious palliative. However, considering the state of the world in general and the black community in particular, most would agree that memory loss and avoidance leave a crumbling cultural and spiritual inheritance for future generations.

There is another option. When events fracture the wholeness of body and soul, the unspoken things, if remembered and reenacted through ritual and liturgy, can become the repository of personal and communal memory. Through ritual, the things that were survived are offered to God in the unspoken belief that reflective and evocative faith practices create a healing space for broken hearts and resilient spirits. However, when intercultural abuses surpass the boundaries of humanity, what is there that can be said? The only appropriate responses to a holocaust after "never again" are silence and shout.

The contemplative moment, whether introspective or charismatic, becomes the expectant waiting for the return to sanity and reason and the spiritual demand for a divine response to the question "Why?" I am suggesting that holocausts can only be approached contemplatively. External responses to unthinkable acts of radical evil, no matter how reasonable, eventually veer toward the demonic. It is inevitable that we become what we hate and replicate what we try to stamp out. There is no response, other than radical love, that is up to the task of healing transgenerational wounds. The healing begins within. Questions that we lay on those inner altars and that receive no response in one generation are handed down to the next.

When you know that this world is not your home because you are deemed to be inferior by virtue of your color, gender, sexuality, or class status, you must look beyond that which can be perceived by the natural eye to find solace. Moses Berry describes this lived transcendence as "always looking beyond the blue."[31] The blue sky was not a roof over their oppression; rather it was a permeable point of reference for prayers and entreaties. For captured Africans, the only safe space for freedom and selfhood was in the mysteries evoked by worship. Psychologist Arthur Deikman contends that mystery can only be entered during a listening or contemplative stance, "a state organized around intake of the environment rather than manipulation of the environment."[32] Accordingly, Deikman infers that the traditional withdrawal and monastic stance toward the world enhances the potential for mystical experiences. The problem with the argument is that nothing we do can lure the divine into that most intimate embrace. It is not the ritual, liturgy, or practice that ensures divine visitation; to the contrary, human receptivity and presence merely ensure openness to this possibility. It is the turning toward mystery, the readiness to receive that prepares the way for spiritual engagement.

The "invisible institution" that E. Franklin Frazier identified as the emerging black church was also a spawning ground for creative contemplative worship, communal prayer, and social resistance. When I speak of contemplation in these contexts, I must necessarily dispel the presumption of passivity and withdrawal from the world. The sense of transcendence that pervades these reports should not be mistaken for detachment. Rather, contemplation during slavery fueled and inspired resistance, rebellion, and escape. In the spiritual microcosms hidden from view stalwart resolve was ignited for those on their way to freedom in the North.

Knee-spots in the Hush Arbor

The final context for crisis contemplation occurs in the hush arbors. Deep in the hollows, under dense brush, the contemplatives gathered. They cleared knee-spots for comfort during the long prayers and songs. Sometime there would be a large washpot or kettle in the center of the gathering to catch the sounds of the pleas. As the spirit inspired ecstatic responses, folks worried that someone would hear, and so they would sing into the pot to "catch the voice" before the overseers heard.

These are the accounts of former slaves who reported on the religious practices of the emerging black church during slavery. The hush arbors are difficult to trace because of the spontaneous nature of the gatherings. Although black slaves particularized this practice, there were also brush arbors that served whites. As a black slave reported, "dey had church under brush arbors and we set off to ourselves, but we could take part in de singing and sometimes a colored person would get happy and shout but nobody didn't think nothing about that."[33] But it is the report of slave-initiated hush arbors as places of refuge and communal worship that is of interest in this study.

> Down in Georgia whar I was born—dat was way back in 1852—us colored folks had prayer grounds. My mammy's was a ole twisted thick-rooted Muscadine bush. She'd go in dar and pray for deliverance of de slaves. Some colored folks cleaned our knee-spots in de cane breaks. Cane you know, grows high and thick, and colored folks could hide de 'seves in dar, and nobody could see an pester em. [Andrew Moss, Knoxville, Tennessee][34]

> We used to have a prayin' ground down in the hollow. Down in the hollow and sometime we come out of the Field, between 11 and 12 at night, scorchin' and burnin' up with nothing to eat, and we wants to ask the good Lawd to have mercy. . . . Some gits so joyous they starts to holler loud and we has to stop up they mouth. I see [folks] git so full of the Lawd and so happy they draps unconscious. [Texas/? Very common][35]

Prayer had to take place in secret. The preparations for the leave-taking from chores and from the watchful eyes of overseers added to the excitement and mystery. The consequences for getting caught were quite severe. The rule of silence prevailed on the days that preceded a meeting in the brush. But when they were all finally gathered in one accord, the pain and distress could no longer be suppressed—tears and shouts were not unusual. In the safety of the community, they began to pray about their situation in cries so heartfelt that heaven itself must have shuddered.

Dwight Hopkins describes the secret prayer meetings in this way: "For blacks, silent moments in the presence of the divine power and grace were supplanted by a total yielding of the self to spiritual possession. To keep silent (that is to keep one's thoughts and joy to oneself) before God reflected a form of individualism in radical contrast to rejoicing in communal activity."[36] Even when life was unbearable, expressions of praise were shared and enjoyed in the secret gatherings.

Ring Shout

In Holy Scripture dance is celebratory worship, an expression of freedom from political and secular oppression, a confirmation of communal resolve. The power of this liturgical form was recognized by the early church leaders in the form of the ring dance. Although ring dances or ring shouts have particular significance for African communities, they were also recommended by Basil the Great, Bishop of Caesarea (c. 329–379); Ambrose, Bishop of Milan (339–397); and John Chrysostom, Bishop of Constantinople (345–407). It was not until Augustine that dance as worship was converted from practice to analogy and metaphor.[37] In all instances, the power of dance was recognized as an egalitarian expression that empowered the community and deepened their connection to God. "Dancing in the Judeo-Christian tradition is associated with the experiences that life is not determined by the past or old self. Bondage to the past may be shaken off by dancing. . . . In the Hebrew Scriptures . . . dance celebrates and effects the end of slavery to the past and beginning of new freedom to act in the world and create [a] new community."[38]

Dance in Africa was the meeting ground for sacred and secular life. Robert Farris Thompson identifies five notable aspects of

African dance: percussion, multiple meters, apart dancing, call and response, and derision. In these various modes of physical expression dancers innovated, created their own steps, acted out social issues, and mocked, satirized, or scorned social practices or persons.[39] During the Middle Passage dance took on new meaning as Africans were forced to dance on slave ships to ensure their viability upon arrival in North America. Slaveholders failed to discern the power of physical movement and often deemed slave dances infantile and primitive without realizing the symbolic and religious significance of the dances. The continuation of ring dances in Africana slave communities connects the diaspora to the early church movements and to their own African tribal history.

"One of the distinctive features of American black slaves' secret religion was the ring shout, probably adapted from African memories. A singer—whoever felt so moved—would step forth from the circle of worshipers. By chanting, dancing and clapping, the community provided a bass beat upon which the singer would create his or her own distinctive musical text."[40] It is difficult to identify the historical origins of the ring shout. Some say that it was a circle dance that may have originated in the Congo. Lorenzo Dow Turner believes that the word *shout* is "a Gullah dialect survival of the Afro-Arabic *saut*, sometimes pronounced 'shout,' meaning a fervent dance around the Kabaa in Mecca."[41] Howard Farrar describes the ring shout as "Africans moving counterclockwise in a circle to the syncopated beat of a drum or drums, moving their heads, arms and legs in a rhythmic fashion."[42] According to Art Rosenbaum, "this is the classic shout step, described by Bess Lomax Hawes as a 'rapid shuffling two-step,' the back foot closing up to but never passing the leading foot: Step (R), close (L); step (R), close (L). The lead foot always advances to the beat of the stick on the principal accents of the rhythm."[43]

The dance is the shout. The accompanying songs and lyrics are layered over the foot movements. It is as if the language of movement can express more than words. In the ring shout, worship replicated the sounds and cadences of the forbidden drum.

David Daniels reminds us that African Americans layered many meanings over the ring shout. These meanings included entreaties to God for deliverance, introspective and meditative movements and songs to prepare the body and soul for deliverance and disappointment, and the celebration of their survival and their belief in God's love.[44] This circle dance was as contemplative as it was evocative. Africans in America were no longer free to enact ritual processionals; as a consequence, the closed circle had to represent pilgrimage and communal resolve. Ritual movement reconnected them to a rhythmic universe and a vibrant African cosmology.

The situations meant to divest them of their humanity strengthened communal ties and personal resolve. Stories of torture and oppression, meant to discourage and create fear, became the grist for storytellers who shared mythic narratives of courage. Even the very tools of torture were divested of their power through inversion and sacred ritual.

Cracking the Whip: A Call to Worship

Suddenly, I am jolted by a loud noise, sharp as a pistol shot. Turning I see that it was the crack of a large whip. Near the doorway and drums, a man is wielding the whip. Unnoticed by me, he has taken it from where it hung on the *poteau mitan*. Now he cracks it repeatedly while moving about near the drums. It dawns on me that this is a slaver's whip. . . . The slaver's whip is here not to frighten the likes of me, but as a sign of the oppression under which Haitians have lived for hundreds of years during slavery.[45]

It is not unusual to visit a monastery or convent where the echo of the cathedral, the harmony of cloistered voices, and ringing bells draw us into a different reality. In Haiti a slaver's whip is the equivalent of a tolling bell during the *Chire d'Ayizan* or the Shredding of the Palm ceremony. This is an initiation rite that focuses on the protection of the place of spiritual birth. Ritual studies scholar Tom Driver describes his observations during the ceremony and the power in the sound of the whip: "as the whip continues to crack, punctuating the drums' own percussions, I begin to feel a certain strength in the room. Having been taken from the slaver's hand, the whip is now wielded ritually."[46] There is no narrative that accompanies this activity, but the sounds and changes of the drum signal the focus of the group. The moment is contemplative because it draws the participants toward memory and spiritual empowerment and because of the ritual inversion. That which has been an instrument of physical and psychic abuse is now the call to worship, a beckoning to the ancestors who have sprawled under the lash, a reminder that "trouble doesn't last always."

We have forgotten the sound of the whip, the crack and whine of its voice as it stroked the skin from children's backs and took the lives of Africans in bondage, one lick at a time. In the hands of the delivered, the whip is an instrument of remembrance, used ritually now because God has been faithful. For many Christians, the words of consecration during communion are sacrosanct: "Do this in remembrance of me." But a whip cracked in remembrance of righteous deliverance is also sacred. The problem is not in the odd use of this artifact of slavery, but in the loss of our own memories of oppression. Listen to this story Blassingame tells, and remember: "I know one man who gave his slave one hundred and fifty lashes in two days, and on the third he died. He crept into the field; and his master supposing he was sleeping, went up and cowhided him, but he was cowhiding a corpse, thinking he was asleep! Such is the condition of slavery."[47] Remember!

The Journey toward Crisis Contemplation

> I'm cracked open now
> No longer drifting
> Running past hate, theirs and mine
> Tipping past "Come here gal"
> toward familiar arms.

I'm cracked open now
looking for myself,
Maybe I spilled into the cleft of the rock
Hiding from the slave catching dogs
Maybe I died trying too hard
To birth my way sane
I'm cracked not broken
Still searching for me
Amid the shards of God's broken heart.

Crisis contemplation emerges in two situations that require ritual lament (the Middle Passage and the auction block) and one instance of ritual empowerment (the hush arbors). Each event is related to the trauma of slavery. Each instance of oppression shatters assumptions about the way the world works. The choices are few when psychological and physical dissolution becomes normative: one can survive or not. But African survival required the reestablishment of intra-communal and spiritual linkages. During the Middle Passage, the moans began to knit the community together across tribal and cultural lines. This is a language that spirits understand. This is a sound that drew tribal strangers toward common purposes.

The crisis of spirit and soul visited upon Africans in the Americas forced them to enter the inner landscape of contemplation, to integrate their fractured meaning structures, and to rely upon divine wisdom. There was nowhere else to turn. The spiritual and emotional tools for survival emerge while the auctioneer continues to accept bids and while the whip is still being wielded. They will turn inward to find safety and solace; they will reorder their value systems to support their survival; ultimately they will shatter into public and private selves, wearing grinning subservience when necessary, undermining the system of slavery whenever possible. W. E. B. Du Bois referred to this split as "double consciousness," a socially fractured psyche, but it is also a creative response to trauma.

Slavery is a crisis of such extraordinary proportions that unless equally extraordinary measures are taken, the result will always be the destruction of humanness. The measures taken by Africans in bondage in the Americas focused on creative adaptation and resistance. If you are locked in a windowless room with no access to the outside, are you a prisoner? Or is a portal always open, an inner door shaped exactly like your hope? You can enter and then journey toward the Creator of all things. As you journey, the chains will still clank, death may even come, but none of that will matter. As Thurman wrote,

> There is a bottomless resourcefulness in [hu]man[ity] that ultimately enables him[/her] to transform "the spear of frustration into a shaft of light." Under such a circumstance, even one's deepest distress becomes so sanctified that a vast illumination points the way to the land one seeks. This is the God in [hu]man[ity]; because of it [hu]man[kind] stands in immediate candidacy for the power to absorb all the pain of life without destroying . . . joy.[48]

Slaves were cracked open mentally and physically to the extent that they lost their ordinary self-understandings. Fortunately, their belief in life continuums, their ritual expertise, and their spiritual resilience allowed them to "absorb all of the pain without destroying joy." The contemplative turn occurs in the midst of trauma and is a crisis meditation that gives birth to a new community. This community contemplatively reorders its priorities and begins the designated task of sifting through God's broken heart for their liberation.

4

Come Ye Disconsolate
Contemplation in Black Church
Congregational Life

We are wired for worship, so we are going to worship something.
—Renita J. Weems

For blacks, silent moments in the presence of divine power
and grace were supplanted by a total yielding of the self to
spiritual possession. To keep silent (that is, to keep one's
thoughts and joy to oneself) before God reflected a form of
individualism in radical contrast to rejoicing in communal
activity.
—Dwight N. Hopkins

There is no understanding of black worship apart from the
presence of the spirit who descends upon the gathered community, lighting a spiritual fire in their hearts.
—James H. Cone

In the African American church we were told to live "holy,
holy, holy," but we were not given the tools to grasp the new
identity.
—Kirk Franklin

Gospel singer Kirk Franklin is correct. Not many of us know how
to be holy. Our expectations about spiritual virtue have little to
do with reality. Holiness can be found in refugee camps, in pris-
ons, and under viaducts. It is as apparent when we are in communion with those who are in economic, physical, or spiritual

peril as it is during liturgy and worship. Examples abound in Holy Scripture of people who launch off into the wilderness without water or provision, apprehensive but believing that God will provide. They mark their doors with the blood of the lamb in belief that the angel of death will pass over, and they journey without maps until the Promised Land is in sight.

What is contemplation if it is not the unlikely lifting of mud, bone, and flesh to the heavens? How is the eunuch in Acts 8:38-39 transported from one place to another? How do the prison walls fall away? These miracles occur not because of resolute spirits, stoically set-aside resolve, and monastic isolation. Rather, it is that which is gifted and blanketed upon a believing community. The spirit descends and the community is lifted. These practices are not unknown to researchers and church folks, but what makes these experiences also contemplative?

I am suggesting that these Africana worship experiences are contemplative because they create an atmosphere for communal listening and responsiveness to the manifestations of God, they impact the ethos and value system of a community, and they heal infected social and psychic wounds. The entry into contemplative practices usually begins with listening for God. Paul Dekar reminds us that listening is a crucial aspect of human/divine interaction. He says, "Jesus couples the word *listen* with an expectation that his hearers will act upon what he is saying."[1] Dekar's examples of scriptural listening include many instances that exceed the boundaries of ordinary articulation and hearing. He reminds us that listening takes on a different character when God's visitations are not limited to orality and the written word. The question becomes, How do you listen when the Holy Spirit descends like fiery tongues or Moses' staff turns into a serpent? What do you "hear" when Jesus walks on the water?

During these times of narrative mystery, all of the senses—not just the human ear and mind—are needed to interpret and understand. It only seems natural for counterintuitive divine messages to be received in equally counterintuitive and mystical ways. Drums welcome God; visitation and prayers become moans uttered by the Holy Spirit in human voice. During public, communal, and powerful Africana worship services, it is not unusual to experience momentary shamanic alterations of ordinary time. When the community steps back into the coexistent ordinary life space, they sing, tell, and testify of joy unspeakable. The mediation of the holy through familiar Africana rites and rituals infuses the sacred into every aspect of everyday life and helps to inform the ethos and values of the community. A good example is found in the African understanding of good and evil. In African societies, it is not unusual for good and evil to be considered equally powerful alternating influences that remain in dialectical tension. One can only tilt the balance by going to the source that set the schema in motion. God's acts in Genesis that separated and alternated darkness and light are not interpreted to mean that dark = evil and light = good. Rather, it is presumed that all things have their oppositional forces, which are without value assignments. They just are. The human task is to flourish in this environment.

To mediate and tilt these forces toward a predominance of good requires communication in the spirit realm. Belief in the mystery of this realm combines with the understanding that there must be a paradigm shift from ordinary discourse and action to inspirited speech and movement. Only through this inspirited communication can ordinary people reach into spirit space and implore God.

Finally, contemplation contributes to the healing of social and psychic wounds. These emotional gashes inflicted by persistent systems of oppression are deep and festering. During the struggle for inclusion, the last thing African Americans would admit was that they had been damaged by America's apartheid. It has taken a while for the realization to set in that education, wealth, consumer goods, and careful enunciation will not open liberation's doors. These are matters of the heart and spirit. Freedom starts as a small ember within; it must be fanned and fed by intentional acts of faithfulness toward God and nurture of self and community. The neglect of one or the other extinguishes the tiny flame. Africana communities in the Americas have found that it takes a village to keep the embers glowing.

That Ole Ship of Zion

"African Americans who gather within the shelter of the black church on Sunday mornings are still far from being free—but the fact that they come to church also means that they are not yet defeated. All come from their various states of oppression with one central question: 'Is there any word from the Lord?' (Jeremiah 37:17)."[2] For the black church the Spirit-led journey toward the land of promise continues. Africans brought to the Americas on ships of death and despair had to construct their own ark of safety. My argument is that they strengthened their communal resolve and survival skills through crisis contemplation. The leaders of the emerging church were shaped and sustained by a unified communal ethos rooted in contemplative responses to oppression. Their relationship with God in the Americas was complex but congruent with their responses to the varied manifestations of God on the African continent. God delivered and God did not; thanks be to the God who is truly free. A free God was a spiritual gift to enslaved people and seeded those same proclivities for freedom in the black church.

From its unstructured beginnings to the mega-churches of the twenty-first century, the black church has been the "ole ship of Zion" that brought the community through the cultural onslaughts of slavery to the outbreak of the Civil Rights Movement. Even though worship moved from clearings in the woods to buildings of wood and brick, the black church is still a hush arbor, a safe space to be in relationship with the community and God.

Within a viable church community the oppression of the wider culture had no power. Class distinctions broke down; porters served with ushers on deacon boards; gender and sexual distinctions became permeable barriers. There were few options. What do you do when the world presents itself as hostile not just to you but also to your community, your orientation, your way of being? How do you maintain a sense of self when that hostility brings forth its own creation—that is, oppression—which manifestly defies the declared "good" of God's created order? Those who are oppressed know intuitively that they are grappling with the forces of social and spiritual malignancy. They also know that no ordinary response will protect them. Those who take refuge in the power of Christian liturgy find unusual models of response to the most impossible situations. The praise teams precede the army (2 Chron. 20:21), enemies share table fellowship, and holiness emanates from a life of servant leadership rather than arcane purity rituals.

James Cone has described the difference between the eschatological hopes of the early Christian community and those of the historical black church community. He wrote, "The post-Easter community expected a complete cosmic transformation in Jesus' immediate return because the end of time was at hand." By contrast, black church communities embrace the theology of a soon-coming Jesus but translate that theological already/not yet immediacy into regular visitations with their Jesus in the midst of song, ritual, and dance.[3] Historically, the expectation was very real that Jesus would save, deliver, inhabit, and—yes—even possess those willing to forsake propriety for the love of God. Something has changed. The expectancy has gone. It is as if we fear the silences and ecstatic moments that might bring listening and memory. Whatever it takes, we do not want to expose the hidden and corrosive unwept tears.

I Don't Want to Cry Anymore!

As Africans in the diaspora, we do not want to remember. Our fear of pain and its acknowledgment has created a church experience that is "drunk on the wine of the world."[4] It is not the music that evokes this critique, but the human-centric worship activities that place more focus on the worshipper than on the worshipped. It is the horrific and inexplicable refusal to recognize the devastation of AIDS in the community, the maniacal consumerism, the willingness to step over the homeless to enter Sunday worship services. Certainly, the music during services is uplifting; however, the rocking incessant rhythms fail to drown out addiction, unemployment, and alienation. We are a people who have forgotten how to lament and repent in community.

Those who visit or attend a black church service during Holy Week will note the difficulty with lament. On the day before Christ is betrayed, the contemplative dirge is de rigueur in many Eurocentric churches. But the atmosphere in most black churches remains inexorably joyful. Calls for solemnity rarely reign in the congregational need for catharsis. Perhaps we are still too historically close to actual lament to embrace its ritual counterpart. A few years ago Rev. Cecil Williams of Glide Memorial Church took the cross down from its prominent place on the altar. This act was in support of Glide's recovery ministries. The pastor argued that a people beset by death and affliction could not bear a constant reminder of the Christian death ritual.

Have we taken the cross down in our individual hearts and in communal worship for similar reasons? Or are lament and silence configured differently in Africana communities? In the Protestant black church the silences are not exclamation marks punctuating the lives of ascetics; rather, in the midst of communal practices and individual experiences the internal silences arise and permeate the worship space. Contemplation erupts, emerges, and shares space with the preacher's cadence and the choir's choral repetitions. Contemplation is the awareness of the unacknowledged angst and hope of the community signaled by the hypnotic humming during baptism and the circle of faithful believers around the sick and dying.

In the words of Thomas Merton, "faith incorporates the unknown into our everyday life in a living and dynamic manner. . . . The function of faith is not to reduce mystery to rational clarity, but to integrate the unknown and known together into a living whole, in which we are more and more able to transcend the limitations of our external self."[5] Merton makes the point that we share the "unknowable" aspect that we attribute to God. Part of the *imago dei* reflected in our lives is the opacity of human interiority. We may be transparent to God but not to one another. Like God, we cannot be known by other people in any total sense. Under ordinary circumstances, human beings are outer-directed, seldom considering their own interiority. We begin to orient ourselves differently when siege and survival become integral aspects of daily life. Worship and congregational life reflect these shifts. Slavery ended, but the siege of racism did not; it just took on a different manifestation.

Something Happened

The magnificence of the cosmos is subsumed in its intelligence and in ours, in its surprising creativity and in ours. In a very real sense contemplation is creation. It is the entry into a space or idea, where the impossible can be shaped, swallowed, and lived. Through a melding of consciousness and devotion, earth bodies and God-givenness become one. Prayers are danced and sung, the air changes, and elements of the life space vibrate with potential and blessed assurance. There is no need to separate from the community, to enter the desert for a closer walk with God. Instead, the in-breaking of the *basileia* of God occurs as sweaty palms grasp and hold, while feet stomp on uneven floors, and while the stickman beats out a rhythm.

This experience of communal contemplation is difficult to describe. Those engaged in the practices cannot tell you much about it, but they usually know when it occurs and when it is being faked. The experiences tell the story. In community there is power: the power may be political and legal, but power in worship communities is also the corporate ability to receive and interpret the gifts of the spirit. The power of contemplation in the midst of the poor and the oppressed becomes the power to bend the social and divine realms in an arc that touches earth and allows earth creatures to reach and embrace what can only be accessed through prayer. This is a powerful witness. James Cone is right when he describes black worship in the following way:

> The black church congregation is an eschatological community that lives as if the end of time is already at hand. . . . [The people believe] that the Spirit of Jesus is coming to visit them in the worship service each time two or three are gathered in his name and to bestow upon them a new vision of their future humanity. This eschatological revolution is not so much a cosmic change as it is a change in the people's identity, wherein they are no longer named by the world but named by the Spirit of Jesus.[6]

I have often wondered what Christian communities expect when they invoke the presence of the Spirit called Holy. Biblical texts indicate that whenever the Spirit was present, *something happened*. The descriptions vary from flaming tongues to Mary's overshadowing. Even the Messiah is driven by the Spirit toward his own vision quest and confrontation with Satan in the desert immediately after baptism. Those who invoke this Spirit can be certain that something will happen. My experiences in various denominational settings highlight this reality.

Contemplation in the Pews

Maundy Thursday is a solemn occasion that precedes Good Friday; it was the highlight of the liturgical year in our Congregational (United Church of Christ) Church in New Haven. In the old sanctuary lit only by candles, familiar members and friends transformed themselves into biblical characters and enacted the betrayal scene with great earnestness. During those rituals, the everyday world was eclipsed by acts of contemplation and drama. However, nothing was more dramatic than my encounter with an apostolic holiness sect in Dallas, Texas.

In the midst of that congregation, contemplation became an accessible mystery. Prophecy, word of knowledge, exorcism, and occasional breaches of the laws of gravity were everyday affairs.

The stone church built by slaves stood on a dirt tract in the shadow of Nieman Marcus in one of the most upscale neighborhoods in Dallas. In this stone edifice I began to consider what it would be like if I entered religious life full-time. Although I was working every day in a bustling legal department, long periods of prayer and fasting changed not only my countenance but my way of interacting in the world.

When spiritually unusual things would happen at the church, those who knew nothing about my life with this group would comment that there seemed to be a light around me. I don't know what to make of this testimony, even though I find similarities with William James's story of a mystical encounter that included "rays of light and glory."[7] Eventually, managers were slipping into my cubicle to tell me about their lives, their beliefs, their trips to Medjugorje.[8] Many sought spiritual advice, although I did nothing to indicate that anything had changed. I still wore normal legal garb, joked, and wrote memos, but something was different.

I do not know exactly what the difference was, but I can affirm each of James's elements of mystical encounter in my own context, beginning with a sense of peace that transcended all situations, a clarity about life that some would deem to be an unveiled perception of "truth," a new vision of a transformed world, and joy unspeakable.[9] When I left the department to join a firm in Miami, this intense spiritual immersion ended. Now I would have to find my way in an environment where the beauty of the natural world competed for my attention.

I became the assistant pastor of a storefront Pentecostal church in Liberty City. This church baptized people in the ocean by Miami Beach and used folding chairs rather than pews. These easily removable chairs facilitated the moves of the Spirit and insured the safety of those flailing under its power. On one occasion I was preparing to preach one of my early sermons—well-prepared but not very inspiring. The praise service had been one long scream. Like maddened cheerleaders, the praise team yelled and hollered until they and the people were exhausted.

When I stepped into the pulpit, I said, "God is not deaf; God hears the whisper of your heart." You could have heard a pin drop. There was dead silence; then the congregation erupted into pandemonium. Now the screams were in support of the theory that God was not deaf. I was perplexed. I like joy as much as any other Christian, and this was a Pentecostal church, but this joy felt desperate. It took a while for me to understand that freedom comes in all forms, and desperation is manifested in incongruous ways. The freedom sought during the days of liberation and "overcoming" had not filtered down to these desperately poor communities in Liberty City.

Oddly enough, freedom denied in the workplace and in society was being recreated in this storefront church. Through prayer, communal ritual, and worship the congregation created the atmosphere for a dance with mystery, an intoxicating embrace of the holy that was so startling and restorative that those who experienced it constantly sought its repetition. The invocation began with charismatic cries and shouts but often ended in the silence and weeping of a stunned community who felt the presence of an accessible God.

In this storefront church, in this place where screams and mystery predominated, there would also be indescribable moments of transcendence. Sometimes the experience came when a church mother stood and prayed in words that began as an ordinary entreaty but then inexplicably lifted the congregation beyond human utterance to a communal bonding with God. Amid the hums and foot cadences there would be an entry into joy unspeakable. Sometimes it would come in the holy dance or the rhythm of the proclaimed word. Always there was a shared sense of transformation. There was also a sense of awe and expectation. Congregants in that storefront church expected God to do something. Commenting on the differences between "high" and "low" church expectations,[10] Annie Dillard writes, "In the high churches they saunter through liturgy like Mohawks along a strand of scaffolding who have long since forgotten their danger. If God were to blast such a service to bits, the congregation would be . . . genuinely shocked. But in the low churches you expect it every minute. This is the beginning of wisdom."[11] Worshippers not only expected the power and danger of proximity with God but actively courted the possibility. Those observing these worship events might presume that they were in the midst of familiar charismatic black church practices. Those involved, however, would have few words to describe the depth of contemplative entry and immersion.

African American contemplative practices are hidden in plain sight. They are enfolded in familiar worship practices from the mourner's bench to the baptismal font, from the church shut-ins to public sit-ins; each of the practices referenced below is grounded in the contemplative religious experiences of Africans in North America.

Transformed by the Dance

Dance has been integral to my discussion of contemplative practices. It plays such a prominent role in the black church because it affords a worshipping community a way to share in the spiritual journey. Our feet mark the rhythms of our lives from labor and play to worship and repose.

> Perhaps one of the main differences between the tribal dance and classical ritualized dance is the way in which the individual evolves. In the tribal dance, individual bodies merge in a rhythmic movement which so to speak takes over all sense of separate identity. The dancer entering more and more into the rhythm of the dance becomes transformed by the dance and no longer retains any sense of being a separate person. Here a group identity replaces and heightens any individual feeling as though it is only through the ecstasy of a corporate tribal sense of unity that the body of each member can achieve fulfillment.[12]

Jyoti Sahi describes this phenomenon within the context of East Indian culture; however, it is applicable in most indigenous communities. As Sahi notes, worship cannot escape the body. Indigenous religions celebrate this fact.

To understand the relationship of dance to Christian faith, one must consider the history of the early church and scriptural references. Although there are only a few references to dance in the New Testament, some scholars suggest that the words *rejoice* and *dance* are the same in Aramaic, the language Jesus and the disciples spoke. If you substitute the word *dance* for "rejoice" in Luke 6:23, you have Jesus saying "Dance . . . and leap for joy." Throughout Holy Scripture, dance becomes a significant worship form when it expresses joy, prayer, or submission to the Holy Spirit. When the prodigal son returns, folks dance (Luke 15:25). Paul reminds us that our bodies are the temple of the Holy Spirit and that our bodies should glorify God with lifted hands (1 Cor. 6:19-20).

Communal dance expressions in the Christian tradition also have roots in Hebrew worship and the entreaty of Ps. 149:3, "Let them praise God's name with dancing." As Doug Adams notes, "the Christian church built upon the deepest understanding of the Jewish tradition of worship by supporting choral dancing, while suppressing individual dancing."[13] For a church deeply suspicious of the body and its appetites, congregational dancing became the safest expression of physical praise. In fact in the Eastern Orthodox Church ring dances were deemed to be the best way to celebrate Easter.[14]

In the black church there is a variety of movement styles. In some traditions dance evolved from the ring shout during the decades of enslavement to the individual expressions of ecstatic "holy dances." For others all movement ended as the adoption of reformed Eurocentric worship styles became institutionalized. Although today the ring shout is ritually performed in Gullah communities on the sea coast of Georgia, most other enactments ended with slavery. People did not want to be reminded of those times or worship styles.

The fact that dance in the black church is ecstatic does not foreclose its contemplative aspects. Some forms of worship are layered in ways that cannot be reduced to a single phenomenon or interpretation. Some people in the community dance for joy with no thought of possession by the Holy Spirit. Some use communal movement as an affirmation of shared spiritual purposes. Others feel the power of the Holy Spirit and offer their bodies for praise. Sometimes one type of dance turns into another. Dance—more than any other form of worship—is bodily prayer, the beginning of pilgrimage from ordinary to sacred space. The body becomes a tablet for the "finger of God." It is not only the head that wants to dwell with God, but also the feet, the heart, and the hands.

The other issue regarding movement in the black church has to do with authenticity. Since the holy dance presumes some level of engagement with the spirit realm, observers who are not as familiar with ecstatic worship wonder how the congregation judges authenticity. In other words, how can the congregation know whether someone is faking possession in holy dance? In my experience, those who are part of the worshipping community seldom try to determine authenticity. I have been in congregations where everyone knew that John or Mary did not have the "spirit" when they leaped into the center aisle to begin their wild dance. Yet nothing was done; nothing was said to stop them. Generally, congregants feel no need to rebuke or judge ecstatic activities. Consider the testimony of evangelist Dorothy Jackson referring to the displays of charisma by some gospel singing groups:

> If the Spirit were to really come to one of them, while they're in this high emotional thing of showmanship—if the Spirit would come and touch them with the meekness and calmness—they'd probably have a heart attack. . . . They would be terrified. Because they would experience the very loss of control they were feigning. And because they would realize, as they felt the deep calmness of the Spirit, the hollowness of their fakery.[15]

Although there is a great deal of tolerance regarding individual worship displays, and a reluctance to inhibit personal expressions of praise, congregants share common understandings about how the Spirit works. They will tell you that God is not the author of confusion; God does not touch us in the same way every time. Consequently, repeated testimonies and actions are suspect. Once again the idea of flow emerges. Glen Hinson recounts the prophetic messages to Oak Grove Free Will Baptist Church in Durham, North Carolina, which were uttered by a prophetess as the word of God to the congregation: "I never come the same. No, I never come the same, for I'm carrying you into things just to teach you how to move with Me—just to teach you how to flow in My Spirit. . . . There are reasons, but they are Mine and I may not always explain them, but just flow with Me. Yes, flow with My Spirit. Yes, flow."[16] If one believes that God's Spirit will manifest in unique ways, then the natural human inclination to control the experience and to interrogate it intellectually is laid aside.

Suffer the Little Children

Children are also part of the worshipping community. Their entry into joy unspeakable is often through play. In a famous song Shirley Caesar tells the story of "playing church" in the backyard with her friends. Part of the game was to feign "shouting" and dancing in the spirit. When her mother saw this from the window, she would sometimes admonish them, saying, "Don't play with God." However, on this one occasion Shirley begins the dance, and then something "gets a hold of her" and she cannot stop. The children with whom she is playing grow uneasy and call her mother. Her mother weeps for joy: she recognizes the holy dance not as a mockery or child's play but as the possession of the Holy Spirit that will lead and guide her for all of her days on earth.

In most historically black churches, it is alright for the children to imitate the adults. They clap and dance and are possessed only with their own innocence and joy. But the adults know that one day something may take hold of them, and it will not be child's play any longer. Formal biblical training takes place in Sunday School or children's church, but not as part of the main service. The altar that draws some children to sit around the pastor for a brief storytelling session or sermonette is replaced by playing church. In charismatic and Pentecostal churches, the children are encouraged to play church (respectfully, as monitored by adults). They may even mimic the preacher and singers, for it is presumed that the altar of the heart will one day draw them nigh. There they will be fed the meat—and not the milk—of the word.

Mourner's Bench: That's Not It!

One night I went to the mourner's bench—I seemed to have the weight of the house on me—and I was in darkness. And whilst I was down on my knees I looked up and didn't see no house-top or sky. I just saw clear heavens and it looked milkish and I said "Lord, what is this?" and He said, "It is love."
—James Albert Ukawsaw Gronniosaw[17]

Back in the day, they had a mourner's bench. My brothers and I would kneel down like the others, but there was always more going on. Sometimes my brother would say, "Nita, look at this," and would jump like he had the Holy Ghost. But Sister Wilhemina would come by and say, "That's not it. Get back down there."
—Renita J. Weems, Mississippi Boulevard Church, Women's Day, October 26, 2003

How do you assess a trans-rational experiential event? How does Sister Wilhemina know that this child is playing and not overcome with the Spirit? The mourner's bench, sometimes called the moaner's bench, was the place where sinners or the unsaved and uncommitted prayed for God's anointing. The bench has been described as twenty to twenty-five inches high, twelve inches wide, and several feet long. Those who were not "saved" sometimes sat on the bench in the front row, where they were certain to feel the "fire" of the preacher's sermon. It was hoped that while contemplating their fate in the next world they might have a spiritual visitation or awakening, or at least a confession of sin and disavowal of sinful behavior.

On another level, the mourner's bench was the portal to participation in communal contemplative practices. It was presumed that those saved and filled with the Holy Ghost would be the holy dancers, the ecstatic singers, those slain in the spirit and uttering prophetic and didactic wisdom for the congregation. If there was any judgment of authenticity, it was based on the willingness of the congregant to confess and be filled. Sitting on the bench was an act of public initiation into the power of community prayer. "An essential feature of Protestant Christianity . . . was the idea that one had to experience conversion to become a full member of the church. Events of great emotional and psychological power, conversions brought about a reorientation of the convert's life."[18] The mourner's bench brings into unity the personal and communal aspects of conversion. Those seated in this place of high expectation will have their conversion experience validated by the observation of the community.

The second phase of conversion, however, involved the discernment of elders as to the authenticity of the experience. This validation process is reminiscent of African indigenous traditions. While the congregation would overlook "playing church," they would not sanction "playing conversion." You might try to fake the experience, but inevitably some elder would whisper to you, "That's not it."

Before conversion these boundaries were vague. After conversion, the convert was deemed to have changed completely. "At that moment, with that experience, they crossed the threshold into a new reality. And the rules in this reality . . . are simply different from those of 'the world.'"[19] As Hinson points out, this transcendent reality is congruent with everyday life. They feel the spirit while driving and cooking; they are healed and receive "blessings" in the natural realm. "Spontaneous and unexpected, the Spirit's visitations frame the saints' 'normal,' cloaking the whole in a mystery that is as much a part of the everyday as every other experience and eventuality."[20]

Hinson notes that since the Spirit can and does visit individuals away from the context of church worship, there must be some value in the communal worship moment. The testimony of worshippers is that communal entries into the spirit realm differ appreciably from normal worship. In congregations that seek and value this experience, the Sunday program is offered in case the Spirit does not show up. When the Spirit is present, a deeply contemplative experience is noted by all. Participating congregants are drawn into a state of heightened personal awareness. This event is attributed to a union of Holy and human spirits. Even after the experience ends, participants are left with an abiding presence, an indwelling Spirit that continues to impart a profound knowing.[21] The mourner's bench experience is a rite of passage that marks full entry into the community of faith.

The focus of the community on the mourner's bench alludes to the mediation of spiritual powers far beyond the control of the individual. In Africana faith and practice there is the understanding that God's presence and relationality are expressed not just in love but also in extraordinary power and danger. Perhaps this explains the preference for contact in the midst of communally mediated rituals.

Contemplating Baptism

There are baptisms of Spirit and of water. It was assumed that after the mourner's bench or some similar conversion experience, you would be baptized by water. Before Spirit baptism was relegated to the domain of Pentecostals, most converts wanted both Spirit and water baptism. Spirit baptism was the assurance that you did not go down in the water a dry devil and come up a wet one. Instead, the convert had a new life in Christ through faith and immersion and the empowerment of the Holy Spirit. For black churches that used full immersion, the presumption was that the convert dies to one life and for a brief moment stops the breath that sustains the body. This symbolic participation in both the baptism and the death of Jesus yields deeply contemplative content for the community. Because ritual enactment overcomes the time span between the historical event and the immediate ritual, it is expected that the Spirit will descend just as it did during John's baptism of Jesus.

When the Spirit descends during baptism, some seekers rise from the water speaking in tongues and flailing under the power. This happens more regularly in Pentecostal and charismatic churches, but it is not limited to these denominational contexts. Although historically some missionaries disdained these emotional displays, others recognized the evidence of the Holy Spirit. "The crowd surged back and forth, and as one bystander would rush to greet a candidate coming out of the water, shrieking forth joy and thanksgiving, the crowd would join in vehement song."[22] The rituals and songs facilitate the entry into this spiritual union and also become the focal point of celebration through ecstatic singing.

The connections between water baptism and the river gods and goddesses of West Africa are in counterpoint and syncretic agreement as the converted enter into the life of the community.

> Religious life was a strong part of the community. Historical traditions brought from Africa (Angola) such as dream interpretation and sharing spiritual folk tales were very important. Many children, including myself, were expected to meditate for several days and share their dreams with the elders before being baptized in the church. It was only through the interpretation of the dreams that one was determined ready for baptism.[23]

Although dream interpretations are no longer integral to baptismal ceremonies, contemplative moments are still important. As the seekers are immersed in the water, which is usually behind the pulpit, the church begins to sing the spirituals that accompany the ritual. Songs like "Wade in the Water" and the "blood songs" such as "I Know It Was the Blood" open the portals to a multiverse filled with sound and energy. To be certain, contained pools that we now use for full immersion differ significantly from the "living waters" in rivers and streams, where baptisms historically took place. Outdoor locations connected the community to the natural realm and its creative blessing and more closely approximated the site of Jesus' baptism. "Directed by both white missionary preachers and black pastors, African Americans went down to the rivers and streams of the South to be baptized. There they found occasion to seal the experience of new life with the extraordinary state of mind of spirit manifestation."[24]

Baptism ceremonies differ among Protestants. Infant baptisms are also deeply contemplative. For those denominations that follow this practice, contemplative connections are made from the child to the ancestors and to the parents, who are to train the child in the ways of God and the community. This is a responsibility that emanates from the spirit realm and is treated with the utmost seriousness. During infant baptism the Spirit is also expected to sanction the ancestral initiation into a community that includes the living and the dead. Christ as proto-ancestor, along with ancestors in the natural family and family of faith, welcomes the child through baptism and its contemplative assumptions into the gathering of a great cloud of witnesses.

Ecstatic Singing: Opening the Heavenly Door

> When I was a little girl, I used to walk to the praise house with my grandmother. And we—when we get there, they start the service. And some of the elders, they lead a hymn. And the ladies, they'll sing spirituals.
> —Doris Holmes[25]

I think singing is the key that open the heavenly door. And
when they start singing, then it look like everything would
open up. Where it was dark, it would be light.
    —Arthur Robinson[26]

On the Georgia and South Carolina coasts, sea island people
remember a time when members of the community used to
cross back and forth "beyond the veil" at will. The praise houses
were simple wooden structures where the community gathered
for prayer. Arthur Robinson is one who remembers. He
describes the opening of the doors of heaven through ecstatic
singing. The whip and lash had no power when the community
could sing of their courage, resistance, and survival.[27]

Songs were not carefully composed and copyrighted as they
are today; they were "raised" by anyone who had a song in their
hearts. Brother Bracey, one of the elders of a Sea Island praise
community, avers, "You told me to sing and I'm doing that too,
Lord, I done done what you told me to do."[28] I have discussed
several communal aspects of the contemplative moment in the
black church; however, I want to be clear that it is not just the
gathering of the community that creates the potential for
indwelling. All must be on one accord before the transformation
takes place. Singing accomplishes this purpose. But it is not just
any singing that creates the atmosphere for transcendence; it is
anointed singing from consecrated singers that makes the difference. "You have some that sing just because they have a voice, or
they're getting good money for it . . . but then you have others
who have really committed their lives to Jesus Christ, and they
walk with Him."[29]

It is the anointing that allows access to the holy, but more
specifically it is the repetition of verses that shifts perception.
There is a point in each choral or congregational song that allows
for the pause and repetition of a particular verse. The repetition
allows individuals to fill in their own story, silently or through the
cries of recognition and affirmation. This is the contemplative
moment, the recognition that each and every member of the

congregation shares the same angst over the troubles of the world and the need for reunion.

The song that began this discussion in the introduction, "Oh, oh, oh, Jesus," offers an excellent example of ecstatic singing. The "oh's" are repeated over and over again until every person remembers a time when they cried out for God's intervention. A deep listening abides between every note and stanza. Those who listen know that the Holy Spirit is in control.

Praying in the Closet and in the Pew

Entreaties to pray without ceasing encode various modes of supplication; however, the black church continued its communal practices during prayer. Sometimes these prayer periods lasted overnight in locked churches as "shut-ins." The community would gather late in the evening to begin a very sparse service that evolved into prayer. During the night, prophetic utterances would come forth; people would pray prostrate on their faces; others would walk the aisles praying softly but audibly; others would sleep.

Whenever I have attended a shut-in, I have been impressed by the intensity of the vigil. In essence, the solitary prayer closet has enlarged. The church takes on a different ambience in the dark. Prophecy would come forth, and a sense of "knowing" would envelop the community. While I was praying during a shut-in in Miami, a song came forth that opened me to a loss that would come within days. Songs are sung a cappella; they are "raised" as people feel led. I heard the words "may be the last time," and I suddenly knew that my beloved grandmother (who was quite healthy at the time) would be making her transition to the ancestors soon. I sat with tears streaming down my face but with a deep sense of abiding comfort and a real sense of her presence. I entered a reverie that I can only describe as a waking dream, in which we communed and said goodbye. A few days later she had a stroke, and by the time I arrived home, she was in a deep coma. My sense of peace came from the time we shared during the prayer vigil.

Years earlier a similar circumstance occurred when my father died. I lived hundreds of miles from home and had not seen him for a year, yet just before his death he kept telling me that I had come to visit him many times during the preceding weeks and that everything was going to be alright. This experience pointed to the permeable boundaries of life and death. The abiding time that precedes death can be deeply contemplative moments in which space-time has no meaning. Boundaries can be crossed at will, granting us the ability to abide with one another in the spiritual landscape that grace allows. If this is true, then perhaps no one ever really dies alone.

On one level, shut-ins allow ordinary people to approximate the experience of "cloistering" themselves overnight. But on another level, shut-ins focus the attention of the community on tarrying. Although prayers can be as diverse as those who utter them, tarrying implies a waiting expectancy. David Daniels describes the practice as contemplative:

> Tarrying parallels contemplative prayer forms that seek communion with God rather than those that seek union with God. It agrees with the forms that stress verbalizing the prayer-word rather than silently meditating. While most contemplative prayer forms limit bodily involvement and movement, tarrying incorporates active, bodily participation. Finally, tarrying is not a private experience of an individual directing him or herself; it is a communal event with the encouragement of altar workers and a prayerful congregation.[30]

According to Daniels, tarrying is prayer that is internalized but communal, fervent, repetitious, and liberative. It assumes a determined and stalwart persistence that is sometimes rewarded with a connection to God and the regeneration of the human spirit.[31]

Each of the practices described represents contemplative inclinations and traditions that are deeply enfolded in the black church. My intent is to highlight and reclaim this legacy. This retrieval must include the first ecumenical church, founded by Howard and Sue Bailey Thurman for the purposes of building a contemplative interfaith community. It stands today as the legacy of this vision.

A Case Study: Howard Thurman's Church Today

On Russian Hill in San Francisco, in the midst of a densely populated neighborhood, is the building that was the site of a great ecumenical experiment, the Church for the Fellowship of All Peoples (or Fellowship Church). There the mystic and contemplative Howard Thurman and his wife, Sue Bailey, began an interfaith worship experience. In the fall of 2002 I journeyed to this place. It was a pilgrimage of sorts. The worship area is up steep stairs. The congregation is small compared to the megachurches that populate most large cities.

To my eye, everything seemed to be in exactly the same condition as it was forty years ago. The dust in the building is thick and seems to be as much a part of the experience as anything else. The pastor and his secretary work from home because of the disrepair of the facility. In an era of multi-million-dollar church budgets, this congregation is not focused on building, repairing, or renovating. They meet each Sunday as if the building is not falling down. After participating in their service I had some understanding of the possible reasons for that seeming lack of concern.

We arrive early and watch a limber gray-haired woman traverse the stairs. The stairs greet you at the door. Climbing them is like climbing a steeper version of Jacob's ladder, but she makes short work of the journey. Her arms are full of flowers that are arranged as we settle into a pew. With only moments to spare before the service begins, she spreads her bounty on the altar with great care and begins stripping leaves and carefully placing the blooms. I am equally careful when I am visiting a church. I try to avoid the ends of pews, because they are usually the exclusive territory of generations in one family. In this instance it probably would not be a problem. The few people who wander into the sanctuary are eclectic.

Howard Thurman would be pleased. Numbers were not his concern. It was the communion of souls that mattered. College students mingle with homeless folks and staid black men and women of former generations. Thurman's contemporaries and friends worship with occasional tourists and strangers. The music is familiar but quiet. The scripture readings placed before the congregation as offerings must be considered and engaged, but they are not dramatic precursors to a charismatic sermon.

Here contemplative practices are given priority. Time is devoted to a guided meditation, which is an element of congregational life that is unusual in black worship. But then, this is not *black* worship—this is just worship. Here there is a dedicated moment of shared entry into the presence of the Divine. The names of God are fluid. No one seems to mind. The quiet that precedes the entry into guided meditation for me is full—mostly full of private concerns that have nothing to do with God or anyone else. I am here to observe, and so my silence is full of my predetermined ideas, judgments, and observation techniques. I am participating, but it is rather in the way that a CNN reporter participates in an event on which she or he is reporting.

But even in my disengaged state the silence persists. Little by little, as I am instructed to breathe in and out, to let go, to enter in, I do. Each of us has been given precious time to release the worries that followed us up the steep stairs, and—to my own surprise—I release mine. In the privacy of this shared space we let the masks slip, just a little. We are not crowded; it is as if we are alone behind our own eyelids, but we know we are together.

The meditation is on forgiveness of self and others. We are asked to think of a time when we needed forgiveness. Because I am so mistake-prone, I have much to be forgiven for and much to forgive. So it is difficult to select a time when I needed forgiveness. There are so many. It is equally difficult to choose a person to extend forgiveness toward. I am sure that I have offended or created disharmony with many. As I rapidly shuffle through a jumble of memories to find a subject, I realize that even this frenetic mental activity is counterproductive.

I hear the voice of the speaker urging us to breathe. And so I stop trying to assess, blame, struggle. I ease into a space where the incidents float before me. It suddenly occurs to me that I have been resisting the guiding. In a society of radically individual individuals, we instinctively reject leading, even as we yearn for leadership. It is then that I decide that I will let this gentle voice guide me. Once the power to determine the scope and depth of this event is relinquished, my breath seems fuller and is released from a much deeper place. When the meditation is over, I feel as if I have been baptized again. I realize that this is heresy to some, but for me it is the ultimate refreshing.

I remember an esteemed professor at my seminary, Dr. Paul Brown, who during worship took a bare branch, dipped it into a water basin, and flung it over the congregation, intoning the words "remember your baptism." It was a defining moment. Because our lives are organized so that we inevitably forget the unforgettable, we must be startled into awareness. The silence had the same effect. I felt baptized into an awareness that made me acutely aware of the bounty of God's love. It was as refreshing as the pentecostal holy dances that ignite my inner fire. The plunge into silence, into reflection and awareness, baptized my noise-saturated spirit. Like a newspaper left out on the patio overnight, I was now covered with the fresh morning dew of God's anointing.

The thing that I remember most is the incongruity: the dust and the fresh wind of the Spirit; the smiles and handshakes of the homeless and of the foremothers and fathers of the Civil Rights Movement. After it was over, I heard the sermon as I have heard few others, primarily because it was spare and unassuming. This word of God emerged out of the stillness of the meditation. It was provocative, and yet, since most of us were still dwelling in the stillness, it was heard from a distance, at the periphery of spirit awareness. I heard the pastor, but I did not. The "amen" affirmation that most black churches rely on to let the pastor know if he or she is doing well was not needed. It was not about the pastor and his homiletical skills; it was about the Spirit of God, and I sensed this in a very real way.

It was odd and wonderful at the end of the service to watch the embraces and connections across chasms of race, gender, and social devastation. In my pew an elderly African American gentleman extended a hand to an Anglo male sitting in the seat next to me. No matter what the older man did, the younger man would not shake his hand. Instead of turning away to end the embarrassing situation, the older gentleman kept asking, "Why not?" with his hand insistently extended. "I can't," the younger mumbled nervously, looking at the floor. "I can't because my hand sweats too much." The older man patted him on the back, and began to walk away, but thought better of it and returned to embrace the young man. How wonderful, I thought. When had I been in a predominantly Anglo or black congregation when the people were so different that this kind of thing could occur?

Everyone gathered downstairs for an after-service breakfast, which was in itself a surprise. Who expects shrimp cocktail, calzones, toasted appetizers, and delicate desserts at a church social? A carefully thought-out kingdom feast had been prepared—perhaps an unexpected feast is a better description. It was a fitting end to feed the spirits of those still damp with the dew of contemplative worship.

Shifting the Emphasis in Worship

Today the Thurmans' church relies on guided meditations and an eclectic congregation to invoke the Holy Spirit. One of the most prominent aspects of worship at Fellowship Church is the shift in emphasis from the "star" preacher to the guided and empowered congregation. The difference between this model of worship and the prevailing model of prophetic charismatic leadership in the black church is stunning. In my opinion the black church cannot sustain itself if it continues to rely on the cult of preaching personalities. At the very least other models of leadership and church organization must provide viable alternatives to an increasingly secular community.

The shift of focus from the worshipping congregation to the star preacher has its roots in biblical and ecclesial history. One can trace this focus on the exhorter to the preeminence of the prophets, the establishment of the disciples as church planters, and the beginning of bishopric succession. Today we are so used to constant entertainment that few realize how closely worship is following those rules of engagement. For those who prefer this worship style, there is nothing more to say. For those eager to revitalize sacred communal time, I suggest a different model of congregational worship.

A shift to the experiential addresses several current concerns: the burnout rate of pastors, the prevalent abuses of power, and the lack of spiritual initiative from the pews. It is a model that takes seriously the "lay priesthood of believers," who bear the responsibility of pastoral care to one another. I have no quarrel with the "call" of specific leaders; however, I am perplexed when a calling morphs into a specialized professionalism that treats spiritual power as rapaciously as the global market and capitalism treat natural resources.

The shift to a new model may not be possible in denominational life. Instead a fresh wind of the Spirit may require the reemergence of house churches and small committed groups whose worship styles evolve as they gather and pray together. However, I do not want to collapse this discussion into a mega-church versus small church battle: there are pluses and minuses on each side. Mega-churches have vast resources that should be available to respond to the needs of the community. Yet the sheer size of a mega-church organization and the increased financial responsibilities required to maintain services and systems may obviate that well-meaning intention. In small churches control is sometimes vested in the hands of a powerful group of people who can thwart the leading of the Spirit and control the direction of spiritual growth through the giving and withholding of tithes.

The model I am proposing can be used in any size church. Eventually there will be an intentional shift from pastoral adoration to shared worship responsibility, but the mechanics of that change should follow a change in the worship format. In the first phase of the shift, guided meditations led by different worship leaders become the focus of the gathered community. Those meditations can follow published examples or be created by the group. If created, they should be written and retained as a resource. The second phase is to develop rituals that address the needs of the community. There can be specific rituals for healing and grieving, for job loss and divorce, and simply for inviting the Holy Spirit into the worship. Time should be set aside for follow-up and feedback. I have seen the difference that rituals make for those dealing with specific life issues. Guided meditations provide an entry into ritual, shifting the focus from observed and staged worship events to introspection and contemplative repose. Finally, a meaningful appropriation of the arts also beckons the community toward reflective repose. Mime, liturgical dance that is intentional and spiritually focused, sacred photography, and poetry open the human spirit in ways that words cannot.

Seeds of Hope

The historical black church is the blessed legacy of the ancestors. It carries with it the seed of contemplative hope and empowerment. In a deeply conflicted and pained society, the black church offers guidance for inner habitation and responsive indwelling. The elements that contributed to its emergence are familiar: a mix of diasporan people from the African continent, the crisis of isolation and oppression, the institutionalization of slavery, and the emergence of a spiritually diverse but coherent community.

This community developed faith practices that combined the cultural significations of African cosmologies and traditions with "white Christianity" taught during slavery. Add to this mix a sociopolitical reading of Holy Scripture that nurtured the activism of the Civil Rights Movement, and we have described some of the basic elements of the black church. It is certainly a beginning, a thumbnail sketch that focuses on the familiar. However, in this book I am seeking more.

We have an ethical responsibility to share creativity and new possibilities with seeking congregants. People resist change in churches, but the contemplative turn is not new. It is the continuation of practices that evolved from the early church through the generations to us. Contemplation has been enriched by its sojourn with sorrow and theodicy; it has been strengthened through activism and postcolonial biblical interpretation. This is the tradition that we have inherited. How shall we bless it and pass it on?

5

Joy Comes in the Morning
Contemplative Themes in African American Biblical Interpretation

> The black experience in America has certainly conditioned black interpretation of the Bible. Even though influenced by oppressive psychological, social, economic and political forces, blacks have displayed a tremendous transcendent spirit that has enabled them to confront the biblical text creatively.
> —Bishop Thomas Hoyt Jr.

During slavery, Africans in the Americas were offered a form of Christianity that did not comport with Holy Scripture or their own indigenous religious inclinations. Its primary intent was to maintain the status quo and to foreclose any ideas about freedom. When they began to read and interpret the biblical text for themselves, they found that the Hebrew Bible was something of a repository of their own cultural history in Africa. Moreover, the New Testament proclaimed liberation for the captives and a new life in Jesus Christ. Through the oratory of slave preachers and their own mother wit, which is a form of cultural discernment, they read liberation and empowerment into the texts.

Afrocentric Midrash: The Art of Griosh

The black church drew upon many interpretive resources as it encountered Holy Scriptures. These options included indigenous religious memory, contextual communal interpretation, and creative syncretism. Taken together, this hermeneutical lens became African diasporan midrash. Midrash emerges from Jewish culture and can be defined as "the creative style of textual interpretation developed by the rabbis of Palestine and Babylonia in the third to sixth centuries C.E."[1] Dennis Fischman makes it clear that midrash is not "a method of exegesis"; rather, it is a way of interrogating the silences and omissions in the text. The intent is to determine which practices will please God. Midrash is also a cultural resource that restores human-divine dialogue, reassuring a captive community that God is still in control and that God has not forsaken them even during the worst of circumstances.[2]

In Africana contexts midrash takes on a different nuance. Because of the cultural divergences, I have coined a different word to refer to hermeneutical skills that are particular to black biblical interpretation. The word is *griosh*, which is derived from the word *griot*, referring to African storytellers, who were also historians and keepers of cultural memory. The sound *sh* is a symbolic marker of the hush arbors where Christian diasporan faith perspectives were honed.

In the diaspora none of the elements of African ritual and communal gathering were allowed. The drums were banned, and meetings for worship had to be secretive. In the motherland griots retained the memories through the public recitation of the stories. Without these gatherings the tradition began to wither. When the community could not gather and the griots could not keep the memories, they ensconced their own stories in the biblical narratives. Because slavery severed extended family ties, each communal group had to have their own methods of maintaining the corporate memory.

During slavery the art of griosh, or interpretative biblical dialogue, was shared by all and became the communal connection that had been lost in bondage. This chapter uses griosh just as one would use midrash, to interrogate the silences and omissions in the text. Like *lectio divina*, griosh is a contemplative reading of Holy Scripture, a method of interpreting the incomprehensible situation of slavery. I have no doubt that it will be equally efficacious in the incomprehensible situation of postmodernity.

The question of biblical interpretation is one that persists in black congregational life. Drawing on the scholarship of Cain Felder and Randall Bailey, Cheryl Kirk-Duggan suggests that black church biblical interpretation often relies upon biblical literalism, eisegesis (reading into the text), and a sociopolitical understanding of biblical calls for liberation.[3] Kirk-Duggan's point is that the black church often avoids critical analysis of the text they so revere. However, this reverence does not impede the critique of dominant culture theologies. A hermeneutic of suspicion has allowed the emergence of liberation themes and the creative revision of textual meaning and praxis. But liberation is not the only motif that emerges from Holy Scripture.

There are also contemplative models throughout the biblical narrative. Sometimes the contemplative is seen in the relationships of leaders and prophets with God. At other times the contemplative arises as a textual invitation to read into the narratives the unexpected potentialities of God the Spirit. From the leaders and prophets of the Pentateuch to the Essene community and John the Baptist and Jesus, those who were engaged with God's presence sought the immediacy of divine relationship through cycles of activism and contemplation.

This chapter considers contemplation in biblical contexts as a hidden treasure for the black church. For the most part, contemplative texts have been reserved for occasions that required the ritual amelioration of sorrow, suffering, or death. In the following analysis, I look at familiar passages using a griosh—creative midrashic methodology—to highlight and interpret neglected contemplative themes in the biblical texts. The following examples taken from scripture illuminate contemplative readings of the gospel.

In the Beginning: The Spirit Broods

When Genesis begins, the earth is a pulsating womb that shelters deep waters and undifferentiated powers of light and dark. Then the Spirit broods and blows, and, in accordance with divine purpose expressed as "Let there be," goodness is declared. Goodness is not superimposed on the cosmos. In the beginning it takes the form of potential waiting for the opportunity to express itself. It is the word, the orality of God, that differentiates and organizes natural phenomena into integrative categories in preparation for the beginnings of an earth community.

When Africana cultures encountered this constructive word in the opening chapters of Holy Scripture, it had to seem familiar to them. As keepers of an oral culture, they revered the words that retained their cultural history and their worship rituals. Here was a God whose words were generative and compelling. It was utterance that caused the earth community to assemble and separated the elements into cycles of meaning not unlike the seasons that marked the lives of those on earth. This ever-present but hidden God called the matriarchs and prophets toward a new reality that required pilgrimage and suffering.

Despite human failings the plan continues to unfold. If it were not so, the story would end with the human exiles peering back at the angels with flaming swords who are guarding Eden. Instead, the narrative continues. This had to be encouraging to people whose pilgrimage took them on a voyage over the deep, whose life categories had been scattered to the four winds, only to be reassembled on distant shores in a confounding way. They would not be the servants of those who assumed ownership of their bodies; instead they would serve this powerful God: "See, then, that I, I am God; there is no god beside me. I deal death and give life; I wounded and I will heal: none can deliver from my hand" (Deut. 32:39).[4] Walter Brueggemann describes this declaration as an assertion of Yahweh's sovereignty. Evil deeds of frail humans pale in the face of such sweeping claims. This is a "Word God" who encompasses all of the attributes of the lesser gods in the West African pantheon, controls nature, and privileges narrative and rhetoric as creation's tools. An oral people encounters an oral God and begins a relationship that will continue through the ages. This is the microcosm that spawns the mysterious underpinnings of faith and deliverance.

Hebrew Bible Contemplations
Exodus and Entry: Pilgrimage and Presence

Lead on Word God, lead on
When you speak the waters of doubt part
understanding dawns,
and shards of hope glimmer.

When you say yoke, we mean bound
You mean easy.
When you say burden we mean heavy
You mean light.
You give manna
we beg stew.

Sear your divine sayings into our rebellion.
Marry us to this living gospel
Lead on Word God, lead on.

Nothing could be more meditative than pilgrimage. The movement toward outer sacred space enhances the sacred spaces within. The Exodus story is a biblical pilgrimage that most approximates the contemplative turn toward inner awareness and divine reunion. Although this is a story of the deliverance of the Hebrew people, it is often linked to black liberation theology. Although there are interesting parallels with regard to the salvific acts of God for an oppressed people, the model has been overextended and overused. It simply cannot subsume all of the holistic and restorative options for Africana people.

To make the biblical narrative fit the story of African diasporan displacement, several contextual elements must be ignored. The Hebrew people make a pilgrimage from the bondage of Africa to liberation. Africans make a pilgrimage from freedom in the motherland to bondage in the Americas. The Israelites regard Egypt as the house of bondage; Africana people regard Egypt as a center of higher learning and the locus of spiritual refuge for Jesus, Mary, and Joseph. Egypt is all of this and more.

Some biblical scholars contend that Africana identifications with this passage may have been so complete because there were Egyptian and Jewish Africans on both sides of the divide. Others rely on the metaphorical aspects of the saga that do not require objective alignments of fact and history. But the purpose of this reading is not to determine the racial continuities or disjunctures between protagonists in the story but to delve into the contemplative aspects of the experience. The Jewish and African communities experienced an event that defied their sense of order in the universe.

As the Egyptians pursue them, Moses and enslaved Hebrew people begin an exodus, which is the bodily enactment of a faith covenant. This is not a romantic act of adoration and trust. Essentially, they have no choice; they cross because they must. There is an army behind them and a sea before them. The walk through the Red (Reed) Sea is not really a faith walk. The Egyptian horsemen are pressing close behind them. They will trust God or die. And so they cross, whether, as some commentators believe, they are wading through reeds or, as our liturgical imaginations would prefer, they are in the midst of walls of water. Whatever the reality was, they have entered into a covenant that wedded them to a God of mystery and power. The meaning of this union is not yet clear.

The exodus is an interesting choice for contemplative analysis. One would think that the very act of displacement would make the centering reunion with God and consistent contemplative practices more difficult to identify and practice. To the contrary, God's presence is evident in the fire and the cloud. Africans familiar with natural phenomenon know that the natural order of things can be amended or supplanted at the will of the spirit realm. The manifestations that occurred before the exodus are clear indicators of God's interventions. When the crossing finally occurs, the people are joyful but stunned. Although they are numbered in the thousands, they cross without any loss of life and now stand safely on the other side, watching the swirling waters claim the Egyptian horsemen.

They are embarking on a journey because God has finally shown up. When Joseph brought his family to Egypt all those many years ago, there was no thought that bondage would be the result. But now God has heard the prayers of the people, and the women want to dance to celebrate the miraculous events of the day. Miriam leads the celebration. The dance that Miriam initiates helps to reintegrate the sense of community that could have been fractured by the shock of the passage. By reenacting the crossing in a familiar dance, Miriam accomplishes several purposes. Dance and song seal the memory of the event in their minds and confirms the power of God; it also celebrates the bravery of the community and prepares them for the journey ahead. The dance with timbrel and song is the beginning of a new pilgrimage. Although the people know of God's feats in battle and the defeat of many enemies, this passage is the first step toward overcoming their own fears of the unknown. Of one thing we are certain, exodus signifies the crossing of a community from a world of linear historical progress and objective time into a metaphysical reality that requires reliance on a Spirit God. Africana adaptations of this story reflect this understanding.

The miraculous aspects of the exodus obviate the need for stillness because anyone who observes the fire and cloud knows that God is present in the phenomenon. But the people do not know what God is up to. Brueggemann captures the relationship of oppressed people in the following spoken and unspoken questions to God.

> *Where now is your God?* Here and everywhere, but in ways one cannot administer.
> *How long?* Until I'm ready.
> *Why have you forsaken?* My reasons are my own and will not be given to you.
> *Is Yahweh among us?* Yes, in decisive ways, but not in ways that will suit you.[5]

The questions are not answered; instead, a belief that God is present has to suffice. What could be more conducive to contemplation than this mix of inscrutability and orality? The contemplative aspect of this biblical reading is congruent with the belief that God has a broad view of history. Although faced with insurmountable odds, human beings can journey on, without provision or plan. They may or may not be delivered together in unlikely ways by unlikely leaders. But when deliverance comes and they have crossed over into the next phase of the journey, they will celebrate, reenact, and remember.

Fiery and Healing Serpents: Look on This

"And just as Moses lifted up the serpent in the wilderness, so must the Son of Man be lifted up, that whoever believes in him may have eternal life" (John 3:14-15). Healing comes from the most unlikely places; in fact, that which has afflicted you may become your salvation. Look on the serpent who deceived you in the garden of Eden, poisoned you in the wilderness. Deciding what is good and evil is the foolish pursuit of humankind. Life is. In it you will have suffering, but some of the suffering will come from what you thought was good. Black church interpretations of this passage rely on a practical knowledge of healing and its sources.

Africans in the Americas were told as part of the sermonic narrative that healing comes from God through Jesus Christ. As many converts will do, they inculturated that theology and interspersed it with their firsthand knowledge of roots and herbs that was their African legacy. Tammy Williams delineates the belief systems of the black church with regard to healing in the following way: (1) God's response to healing is varied and often counterintuitive, (2) our bodies provide a dwelling place for the Holy Spirit, (3) we have a Christian duty to care for our bodies so that we can continue to glorify God, and (4) effective ministry requires a healthy body.[6]

The first two tenets are ensconced in the heart of black church ideology; the last two have been sadly neglected. In the traditions with which I am familiar preventative health care is not first on the list. The black church has not decided how to resolve the conflict in biblical language that, on the one hand, designates the

body as a disdained site of sin and, on the other, touts the body as
a potentially holy temple for a residing Holy Spirit. The confusion results in the body and its needs being ignored until catastrophic events occur. In this particular text the catastrophe
comes in the form of stinging serpents; the remedy comes in the
same form.

Most commentators focus on the image of the lifted serpent as
a "type" of the lifted Savior. In Africana contexts the snake would
be very familiar as a symbol of divinity. In Igbo culture "Chi-
Ukwa is the creator who bestows life force, death, and rebirth.
This force can manifest itself through the royal python, *eke*. The
python is revered and protected in ways that are quite distinct
from Judeo-Christian beliefs."[7] But what is contemplative about
the serpent?

The contemplative aspects of this scripture emerges from particular modalities of healing. While Africans in the Americas
would have known the procedures for root remedies that require
gathering and preparation, the only requirements for God's healing is the cessation of complaint and compliance with a decree to
"look" at a symbol of the serpent. In the text the people are dying
from snakebites, and they are told that the source of their healing will come from the source of their suffering. This God is
clearly the source of all things. Blessing and curses emanate from
the same ordinary creature at God's command. Gone are the fan-
tastic and dramatic phenomena of Exodus—of rivers turning to
blood and frogs raining down on the landscape. Now a simple
faithful glance will do. Thomas Merton says,

> The way to contemplation is an obscurity so obscure that it
> is no longer even dramatic. There is nothing in it that can
> be grasped and cherished as heroic or even unusual. . . .
> There is supreme value in the ordinary everyday routine of
> work, poverty, hardship, and monotony that characterizes
> the lives of all the poor, uninteresting, and forgotten people
> in the world.[8]

There is power in the ordinary, enlightenment in obscurity, and
healing at the very center of the pain. Here the text offers contemplation and obedience as sources of healing. The serpent is

only the point of focus: it is the faithful contemplative gaze that
becomes the conduit for God's grace. This gaze must focus the
attention of the community. It is not the afflicted who are
required to contemplate; rather, it is the gathered community,
bitten and not bitten, who must look.

I have chosen this scripture, even though it is not one of the
favorites of the black church, because it offers a pericope that
falls within the communal contemplative healing tradition. In a
community beset by diabetes, heart disease, and high blood
pressure, the inability to center spirituality through and in the
body creates catastrophic alienations of cell and spirit. For those
who neglect the body, the contemplative moment may come as
the body declines. Then the truth of who and whose we are sur-
faces in the midst of physical weakness.

So many paths lead toward enlightenment. We can dance into
God's presence in healthy bodies, offering our shining temples to
the Most High, or glow on our sick beds shining through the
shackles of disease. Each act is offered in defiance of an earthly
order and in reaffirmation of the Spirit of God within us. There
are many options along the spectrum, but the optimal contemplative stance is fully embodied. Our rational ideas as to the
source of our healing will always be inadequate. In response to
our incessant "need to know," the Spirit lifts the serpent—even
while we are still smarting from its sting—and whispers, "Look
on this."

In the Fiery Furnace: Shadrach, Meshach, and Abednego
The story is familiar: the Hebrew boys will not participate in
false worship. Instead they are willing to be committed to the
fiery furnace, heated seven times hotter than it has ever been—
so hot, in fact, that those charged with the responsibility of toss-
ing the Hebrews into the flames die doing their designated
duties. This may be one of the favorite biblical stories of the
black church. The focus is on the relinquishment of control to a
higher power, the willingness to be committed to fire rather than
disobey God. In the interpretive context of the slave tales "Br'er

Rabbit" and "The Tar Baby," the fire is the brier patch. Although it seems to the enemy like the perfect site for our demise, it is a familiar and God-empowered sanctuary. In the midst of the flame, at the catalytic center of the heart turned inward, is redemption. But even if redemption does not come, the belief is that God will be faithful.

The black church recognizes the contemplative moment in the midst of fire more clearly than in any other narrative event. Like the three Hebrew men, people in the black church are also bound and tossed. The scripture says that Shadrach, Meshach, and Abednego were "bound, still wearing their tunics, their trousers, their hats, and their other garments, and they were thrown into the furnace of blazing fire" (Dan. 3:21). One wonders why the system requires this binding with clothes. Griosh supplies the missing reasons: the system must bind so that it can see the ineffectiveness of its feeble shackles. For within the next few verses they are unbound and in the presence of God. Daniel 3:25 describes the events dramatically: "I see four men unbound walking in the middle of the fire, and they are not hurt; and the fourth has the appearance of a god."

The binding is the important contemplative element in this passage. For even when bound in prison, like Paul, the Hebrews, or men and women of color today, one like the Son of God can come and abide with us. This is the quintessential contemplative moment. Jesus comes and abides but does not release. It is the system that releases. The system must undo what it has done, but until it does, one can sojourn with Jesus. When the system bids you to leave the fire, it will be as if you have never been in the heat. No fumes, smoke, scorch, or ash. Who would have thought that contemplation is a safe haven even in the midst of the flame?

Hagar and Ishmael: A Theophany in the Desert

"Have I really seen God and remained alive after seeing God?" (Gen. 16:13b). In the years to come, the desert would be the place of refuge for Africana Christians in Egypt and Ethiopia, but this story finds us in an odd situation. What does contemplation mean when you are exiled and awaiting death? Hagar is a popular figure among womanists and ethnic theologians. She completely embodies marginalized women who have been exploited by religious and secular systems. When dissension arises between Sarah and Hagar, Hagar and Ishmael are sent to the desert. This wilderness is not unlike the place where John the Baptizer ministered and where the Spirit of God leads Jesus to the tempter to test his call to ministry. The desert is a place of renewal, but it is also a place of death.

Perhaps having heard the stories of God's miraculous interventions from Abraham and Sarah, Hagar expects this miracle-working God to appear. There seem to be no other options. When nothing happens, Hagar pauses for a moment to contemplate their fate. It is in this moment of stillness that God meets her under the tree. "Hagar has a theophany. . . . She becomes the recipient of a promise made by God. The promise is identical to the promise given to the patriarchs by God."[9] John Waters suggests that Hagar is the first non-Israelite matriarch, a woman from North Africa who receives a promise of descendants and land.[10]

Waters questions Hagar's presumed servile status. There is not enough data to definitively determine whether she was free, slave, or part of some undesignated part of the household. However, he believes that the King James Version of the Bible and the racialized predilections of the interpreters were imposed on the text. But whether she is slave or free is not the only question that arises in the text. The other fascinating element of the narrative is that Hagar's contemplative moment moves her to boldly name God. Phyllis Trible and Delores Williams note that instead of referring to God using the names of the patriarchs, she names God herself.[11] "So she named the LORD who spoke to her, 'You are El-roi [the God who sees]'; for she said, 'Have I really seen God and remained alive after seeing him?'" (Gen. 16:13a). This is surprising because she knows the traditional names of God: she has been part of Abraham's household for a while.

Out of her contemplation comes the ultimate inculturation of God's presence. She is Egyptian and also knows the creation stories that attribute human life to the tears of the god Ra. Ra creates with his eye; Yahweh also creates hope and a future for Ishmael by seeing her plight. This seeing God answers prayer but not in the redemptive and liberative way that we expect. Hagar is sent back into a potentially abusive situation. All she has is the promise of God and the unbelievable experience of a personal encounter. Was it enough to sustain her as she returns to the Abrahamic household? Is it enough to sustain us today? In an era where abuse runs rampant throughout the black community, destroying the lives of women and children, can we use God's solution as a model for others in this situation?

In this instance, God's protection can be reasonably implied in the promise. In order for the promise to come to fruition, Ishmael must survive, marry, and have children. We know that this occurs because later Hagar arranges his marriage. But survival is as rooted in the ordinary as it is in God's miraculous interventions. After Hagar's encounter with God, she is changed. No person can experience God's presence and remain the same. A change in her spirit would ultimately change her relational circumstances. So although she goes back into ostensible bondage, her time of contemplation with God under the tree has freed her spirit forever. There is no longer a need to taunt Sarah or to respond to Sarah's taunts. Hagar has heard from God that she will be sustained.

There is much contemplative fodder to mine from this narrative. First, entry into contemplation presents the possibility of a freeing encounter with God, a rare theophany, and God's abiding presence. Second, Hagar's prayers bring her into direct contact with God's love in all of its intensity. When Moses has the same encounter, his face glows. Hagar claims to have "seen" the God who sees her. Does she return to Abraham's household glowing? If so, that would be sufficient to guarantee her protection. If she is not glowing on the outside, is it because she has seen God with her inner eye during contemplation? God's passing over her heart and mind would ignite a sustaining inner fire. "Love has not only the virtue of uniting without depersonalizing, but in uniting it ultra-personalizes."[12] The black church can draw from this pericope the reassurance that in contemplation we meet the God who promises without regard to cultural or spiritual entitlement. When Hagar returned to Abraham's camp, night had fallen, yet all could see the light of God shining 'round about her.

New Testament Contemplations
Pondering Mary

The song from black church tradition "Mary Had a Baby" speaks to the bottom line. Notwithstanding angelic pronouncements, the surprise of Joseph, and Mary's silent pondering, a baby is on the way. A Savior who has a mother is something to contemplate. A mother who ponders is someone to emulate. *Pondering* is a heavy and introspective word. Bonnie Miller-McLemore says, "The sonorous effect of the word is magnified by its location in the heart rather than in the mind. This location . . . deepens the wisdom found within and through one's passions. Keeping thoughts in one's heart means keeping them at the center or core of one's being."[13] This is the contemplative prayerful model that is so important for the postmodern church. The Marian tradition that can inform black church spirituality is ensconced in her prayerful acceptance of God's plan, even when only a small element of that plan was revealed to her. "Prayer that waits, that is persistent, and that is practiced in common is the prerequisite of the effectual ministry of the church."[14]

The church of the twenty-first century is not called to be a model of corporate organization but rather an organic and responsive body of Christ. Trusting God through a virgin birth and the death of God's beloved son is trust of the first order. The events unfold in ways that defy human rationalization. The journey that Mary is on is unusual. Not only is she pregnant as the result of a deeply contemplative overshadowing, but in time she will find herself at the foot of the cross with her friends pondering yet again. A trio of Marys witnesses the sacrifice of the Messiah, whose divine accessibility and vulnerability are the unexpected gift to humankind. Thereby the pondering is multiplied by three, a feminine trinitarian symbol that has been overlooked in biblical interpretation.

The black church has accepted its role in the liberation story of Africans in North America, but it has not claimed its Marian role as mother and witness to the working of God here on earth. As mother its first call is not to church growth but to the birthing and nurturing of the Christ imaged in the least of us. As witness of God-with-us the church is called to stand silently at the places where the national powers are crucifying the innocent, and waging war against the poor. At the foot of the cross the risk to the three Marys was great. The men knew this as they fled, but the Marys remained, willing to embody a contemplative resistance, which is simply the expression of love and faith that transcends the ability to see or understand the outcomes.

A Contemplative Jesus: Gethsemane Prayers

In the garden of Gethsemane the Jewish lament tradition becomes the discourse of inquiry and obedience. As Walter Brueggemann notes, lament is the language of prayer in the mouths of people who believe that God will answer, hear, and respond. They are "real prayer[s] prayed in real hope to a real God who makes real answers."[15] Jesus knows that sacrifice is required but still asks out of the depth of his humanity for the "cup" to be removed. Howard Thurman speaks to this profound moment: "It is not merely that at his age, he didn't want to die . . . but to die with such a sense of 'my work not done.' And if I can convince myself that no one else can do the work, then death is a terror."[16] Thurman concludes that "Jesus is dealing with the most difficult thing in religious commitment: To be able to give up the initiative over your own life; to yield at the core of one's self, the nerve center of one's consent to God; and to trust the act itself."[17] When the answer does not come, Jesus responds to the silence out of the depth of his divinity and out of the confusion of his humanity: "Your will be done" (Matt. 26:42).

In this pericope we see the difference between sleep and prayer, boundaries that are often blurred in the prayer life of a church focused on activity rather than repose. The disciples' response to Jesus' request that they contemplate and pray with him is not unlike our own. They begin and intend to abide with him, but they fall asleep. Jesus chastises these foundational members of the church by warning them that the betrayers are at hand and this is no time for sleep. As the language of Christian grace is co-opted to serve the needs of nationalism and consumerism, the church is warned to awaken from its lethargy. Only the discipline of contemplative practice will prepare us for the time of crisis when Jesus calls for the community of God to arise.

In a very real sense this narrative reminds us that contemplation and prayer are attitudes of watchfulness. We are most alert when we are in a prayerful attitude. As a culture we have been taught to rely on our processes of thought and reason. We make decisions based on deductive processes; Jesus turns inward for answers and beckons us to follow.

Simon of Cyrene: Cross-Bearing

Sometimes abiding with Christ requires the sharing of burdens and blessings so mixed and complex that the effect is staggering. Some commentators suggest that Simon of Cyrene was an African Hellenized Jew whose sons, Alexander and Rufus, are referenced in Mark 15:21. The contemplative aspect of this passage emerges from the overwhelming aspect of his task. Because the cross is too heavy for Jesus to bear, Simon must carry it. Some commentators wonder why Simon was nearby. Was he actually a bystander, or was he a follower of Jesus who like the three Marys stood near rather than far away? Antonious Conner suggests that Simon was a disciple: "It's quite amazing about an African helping Christ carry the Cross. He did not just happen to be there on the day of crucifixion, for he was a follower and a disciple. He was part of a vibrant movement of Africans who believed in Christ and were living in Jerusalem at that time."[18] Stephanie Buckhanon Crowder disagrees. Using cultural studies as an interpretive framework, Crowder argues for a case of Roman conscription. In her analysis, Simon of Cyrene is the stranger compelled by the Roman authorities to carry the cross of Jesus.[19]

How do you respond when you are asked to do what the Savior cannot? This is the one called Yeshua the Messiah, the one who came to save and redeem. Yet he staggers in the dirt as you move into place and lift the solid wood to your shoulders. As you bend under the weight you realize that this vulnerable God is totally human even as he is completely divine. He looks at you and smiles with such love that you no longer feel the pain. There is a contemplative rhythm to your movement, a silent dialogue with each step. Without saying a word, you are caring for each other.

Extreme burdens alter the human psyche. When the body is subjected to torture or extreme duress there would seem to be no option for contemplation. This is only true if contemplation is considered to be a purely reflective activity. If, however, contemplation can be fully embodied, then a walk under the staggering weight of the cross is the quintessential meditative act. It is not merely carrying the burden of another; it is also the risk of association, the proximity to those ethereal boundaries of life and death, and submission to the authority of the powers. The powers of institutional depravity are never so dangerous as when they believe that they are crushing innocence to protect the status quo. Under such circumstances, no one is safe.

This pericope models the true nature of servant leadership. Here Simon the African suffers as a servant as he shares the burden with the Suffering Servant. If he is not a disciple before this act, he is now, for he is walking with Jesus in ways that none of the others have. He is a parabolic symbol of how the church should lead. The people with Jesus at the end are not the clearly identified disciples (learners who never quite seem to learn) but rather the people whose insight and understanding have been sharpened by their ostensible powerlessness in the culture as a consequence of race, class, and gender. At this crucial moment it is the African who silently accompanies Jesus to Golgotha and the women who silently stand at his feet. These are his closest contemplative companions.

Pentecost: This Is That!

All of the business has been handled. A new disciple, Matthias, has been selected by lots to replace Judas. And now they are gathered "on one accord," waiting and praying as the Spirit descends in a dramatic way—like fire, like tongues, like nothing that their intellectual capacities can grasp. This is not a thought event: it is a doing, being, bodily possession event. The spirit is giving them the ability to speak "in other tongues"; they are barely able to stand under the anointing. As they stagger about, observers wonder whether they are drunk. What kind of contemplation can be mistaken for drunkenness?

Peter, the disciple who ran away during the crucifixion, the man who was too afraid to finish his walk upon the waters with Jesus, steps out before the crowd to explain that "this is that" which was promised. Contemplation always involves some mix of reality and transcendence. In this instance the Spirit's appearance completely displaces the ordinary, and their God-empowered proclamation is recognized by the people. But the people are so distanced from the practices of contemplation that they do not recognize the disorientation of the disciples' bodies as a direct response to divine presence. Yet the speech that emanates from this profoundly contemplative moment will seed a new missional initiative and raise questions as to the nature of spiritual outreach activities.

During Pentecost, missional activity is a natural outgrowth of sacred empowerment. In our own context missional activity often includes an overriding denominational and political agenda. One need only go to the continent of Africa to see the incongruities lived out as Africans imitate the style and dress, music and liturgy of their European benefactors and colonizers. A message of salvation clothed in denominational western epistemological interpretation is not the same message of Pentecost. The heavy-handed displacement of African pantheons with a western theological perspective is self-serving. But even more problematic is the belief that we are right and that our image and understanding of God supersedes all others. The message of Pentecost is different.

It erupts out of the contemplative unity of the gathered community. From the realm of multiple realities, the Spirit storms the upper room and disrupts the probability of institutional dysfunction that is certain to follow Christ's leave-taking. Instead the disciples are left with flaming tongues and a burning message. Is there a Pentecost for our generation that will free us from the structures and vain assumptions that bind us?

Reading the Bible through a hermeneutical lens that includes griosh, historical memory, and experiential data creates space in the narrative for our own stories. The events depicted in scripture are not flat accounts but apertures in the everyday world. Entry offers resources for sustaining ministry and correctives to egocentric exegetical presumptions. The Holy Spirit is a text that can only be read when the human spirit brackets its limitations in exchange for inner sight and "this is that."

6

Ain't Gonna Let Nobody
Turn Us Around

Contemplation, Activism, and Praxis

Each generation leaves a legacy to succeeding generations. . . .
That legacy may be solid, etched in stone, or it may be as fragile
as a house of cards, tumbling in the first gust of wind.
—Barbara Jordan

At the heart of the universe is a higher reality—God and
[God's] kingdom of love—to which we must all be conformed.
—Martin Luther King Jr.

The authentic mystic can never flee the world. He or she must
resonate with the suffering and agony that is the common
legacy of humankind . . . and active mystics who live in the
hurly-burly enter into the same inner silence as those who live
in the desert.
—William Johnston

In Afro-American spirituality there is no contradiction between
contemplation and social action. There is no contempt for the
world, but contempt for the world as it presently is.
—James A. Noel

The world is the cloister of the contemplative. There is no escape.
Always the quest for justice draws one deeply into the heart of
God. In this sacred interiority contemplation becomes the language of prayer and the impetus for prophetic proclamation and
action. Martin Luther King Jr. and Rosa Parks were classic con-

templatives, deeply committed to silent witness, embodied and performative justice. The type of contemplative practices that emerged during the Civil Rights Movement became dramas that enacted a deep discontentment with things as they were. For years the black church nurtured its members in the truth of their humanity and the potential for moral flourishing. Worship practices and songs like "You Got a Right" ritualized liberation and reminded denigrated people of God's promises.

As with all great social justice movements, there came a time when worship practices and communal resolve coalesced, and an interfaith, interdenominational, interracial community formed. The commonality for this dissenting community was the willingness to resist the power of apartheid in the Americas with their bodies. This intercultural resistance coalition had to overcome not just the external evil but also the evil that had been internalized. Among people of color, issues included anger, self-hatred, and oppression-induced lethargy; among members of the dominant culture the lust for power and an ethos of control and imperialism skewed relational possibilities.

And yet a community committed to justice formed. It was in many respects similar to the *communitas* gathering that Victor Turner's research revealed.[1] A community is not always an intentional gathering of like-minded people who munch on coffee and donuts as they assess issues of common concern. Sometimes communities form because unpredictable events and circumstances draw people into shared life intersections. Those trapped on planes and in towers on 9/11 became instantaneous communities as they faced death and struggled with cell-phone goodbyes. Their individuality is not lost as we remember them, but their identity is contextually grounded in a shared life experience that I would call community. Communities form when ego-focused concerns recede in favor of shared agendas and a more universal identity. These relationships need only hold together briefly before transitioning into other forms; however, while they are intact, all concerned are aware of the linkages of interior resolve that are at work.

Identifying the Power Source

Most attribute the power of the Civil Rights Movement to the institutional black church. This is only true in part. Clearly, the black church was the womb that nurtured the hope of that social eventuality, but the spark that ignited the justice movements did not come from the hierarchical institutional black church. Rather, it was the quixotic and limber heart of that institution, its flexible, spiritually open, and mystical center, that ignited first the young people and then their elders to move their symbolic initiatives from ritual ring shouts to processional and contemplative marches. "The universal self continually surrenders itself to love. Not in the sense of restrictive or slavish one-on-one connectedness, but in rarefied giving of ourselves in contribution, service, devoted and disciplined acts."[2]

The formation of community during the Civil Rights Movement was the quintessential coming-of-age story for Africana people. During a particular time in history, nonviolent initiatives seeded with contemplative worship practices became acts of public theology and activism. Activism and contemplation are not functional opposites. Rather, contemplation is at its heart a reflective activity that is always seeking the spiritual balance between individual piety and communal justice-seeking. I am suggesting that the genesis of the great justice movements of the twentieth century emerged from the consistent contemplative practices of those seeking liberation. This premise is supported by recent history, from the passive resistance of Mohandas Gandhi, Rosa Parks, and Martin Luther King Jr. to the social protests of Daniel Berrigan, Fannie Lou Hamer, Malcolm X (El Hajj Malik El Shabazz), and Nelson Mandela. Each social stance is linked to the stalwart interiority of visionary individuals and their co-laboring communities.

Since the Civil Rights Movement wound down and equal opportunity for all became the prevailing social presumption, the Africana community in North America has been hurtling toward potential destruction and transformation. I suggest these two sociospiritual destinations not as polarities but as a motley mix of undifferentiated options that tug the community "every which way but loose." Every gain is seeded with just enough destruction, personal and communal, to deflate and nullify the overall sense of accomplishment. Each failure carries upon its horizon the hope and "overcoming" determination of the ancestors that cannot be denied even in the midst of abandonment of social goals in favor of consumerism, crime, and the skewing of moral values.

To be certain, the desire to prove self-worth and wipe out a history of oppression in one generation has taken its spiritual toll. The weariness I encounter is so pervasive and so deep that it cannot be assuaged by the usual liturgy and shout. Something more is needed in the spiritual lives of Africana people. I am proposing that this "something" must include a healing reclamation of a unique Africana contemplative heritage, its communal rituals and practices both silent and oral.

Even in its most passive aspects, contemplation plugs the supplicants into the catalytic center of God's Spirit, into the divine power that permeates every aspect of life. In this space there are no false dichotomies, no divisions between the sacred and the secular. James Noel makes the connection between black spirituality and social action very plain: "any spirituality which does not engage in justice is unbiblical and only reinforces the political and psychic structures of oppression."[3] Noel infers that the very essence of Christianity is its moral plumbline, its mandate to "do justice." Through acts of contemplation individuals and congregations enter the liminal space where the impossible becomes possible. The liminal vantage point described by Victor Turner offers the ability to "see clearly," to critique the prisms of oppression reflected even in the victims. Those privy to this perspective can "reconfigure the status quo with hope, and then . . . implement hope with social action."[4]

From a Christian perspective, the quest for justice begins with participation in the claim that we are redeemed by a suffering Savior. Mel Gibson's graphically violent depiction of suffering in

The Passion of the Christ was controversial for many reasons, including its anti-Semitism. However, it also challenged antiseptic Protestant views of the crucifixion. In theological circles the suffering that precedes redemption is interpreted as an emotionally distant but efficacious moral example, as a meaningful liturgical moment worthy of reenactment, as an ancient historical reality, or, in the case of many Africana congregations, as a present and accessible portal to the current and immediate suffering of the community. This immediacy lends itself to personal and communal transformation through the mystery of spiritual union.

In the words of Simone Weil, the person whose "soul remains orientated towards God while a nail is driven through it finds himself nailed to the very center of the universe; the true center, which is not in the middle, which is not in space and time, which is God." Weil goes on to say that "without leaving the time and place to which the body is bound, the soul can traverse the whole of space and time and come into the actual presence of God."[5] It is in this presence that the path forward becomes clearer and the implementation of spiritual energy is directed.

The activism that ignited the freedom movements had contemplative practices at their center. The very act of passive resistance can be described as stillness in the midst of turmoil, a willingness to subject the body to the chaos of abuse and social rejection while uniting the ultimate purposes of that resistance to the Holy Spirit. Incredibly, abuse loses its power when it confronts the unified resolve of a community and the personal commitment of its individuals. All throughout the history of segregation in North America and around the world, people of color died at the hands of the dominant culture. The meaning of these deaths seemed to be swallowed by time without affecting the policies of those who assented to the deaths and without awakening those killed and their kin to the power in nonviolent resistance.

When killers kill with the state as a silent partner, when "the killed" see no end to the progressive annihilation of spirit and soul, both succumb to a spiritual disorder. This spiritual disorder is most often characterized by flight—flight from prayer, from intimate relationships, from silence and the potential to hear a divine blessing or rebuke. The only spiritual recompense seems to be that eventually societies that sanction violence against the poor and oppressed inevitably ingest the bile they spew and reap the violence they commit. Further indication of our connection to an embedded divine wisdom arises in our realization that whether we want to or not, we recognize the humanity of other human beings even if our hands are shaping the rope to lynch, even if our fists are formed to strike a spouse.

The question is whether this recognition floats through the consciousness untethered or whether it is deeply rooted in spiritual disciplines that imply the possibility of repentance or redemption. Our postmodern societies seem to have found the balm in consumer practices, noise, sports, video games, and reality shows. But even in the midst of the din, a soul in ecstasy will recognize moves of the spirit.

We Are Marching to Zion, Beautiful, Beautiful Zion

The civil rights marches were contemplative—sometimes silent, sometimes drenched with song, but always contemplative. This may mean within the context of a desperate quest for justice that while weary feet traversed well-worn streets, hearts leaped into the lap of God. While children were escorted into schools by national guardsmen, the song "Jesus Loves Me" became an anthem of faith in the face of contradictory evidence. You cannot face German shepherds and fire hoses with your own resources; there must be God and stillness at the very center of your being. Otherwise, you will spiral into the violence that threatens you. What saves you is the blessed merger of intuitive knowing with rationality, pain, and resolve.

The marches for civil rights were contemplative processionals, moves of the spirit "for such a time as this." Like a spiritual earthquake the resolve of the marchers affirmed the faith of foremothers and fathers. Each step was a reclamation of the hope unborn. Each marcher embodied the communal affirmation of already/not-yet sacred spaces. Ronald Grimes describes ritual processionals that bear many of the markers of civil rights marches: "A procession is the linearly ordered, solemn movement of a group through chartered space to a known destination to give witness, bear an esteemed object, perform a rite, fulfill a vow, gain merit, visit a shrine."[6]

Applying Grimes's elements to civil rights marches, I find that the spiritual destination of these justice processions was the consciousness of the nation, the witness was that nonviolence was the most powerful weapon within human control, the esteemed object was the sacred *imago dei* in dark bodies. The rite was the act of walking in community to challenge the forces of evil and death; the vow was the unspoken commitment to redeem the sacrifices of the ancestors. The shrine was within; the merit was God's favor extended to people of faith and obedience. These contemplative acts moved the community toward the fulfillment of one small aspect of the beloved community: the end of legally sanctioned segregation.

The sacred act of walking together toward justice was usually preceded by a pre-march meeting that began with a prayer service, where preaching, singing, and exhortation prepared the people to move toward the hope they all held. This hope was carefully explicated by the leadership as a fulfillment of God's promises. As a consequence, the movement that spilled from the churches to the streets was a ritual enactment of a communal faith journey toward the *basileia* of God.

Protestors through their silence and songs would amplify their humanity for the world to see. As Grimes notes in his discussion of ritual practices, "processants do not occupy centralized sacred space. Instead, they carry their 'center' with them" as they move toward their destination.[7] Although Grimes presents processions as affirmations of established beliefs, as in a pilgrimage or the confirmation of "established hierarchies and order," there is the potential for inversion.[8] Grimes appears to see inversion in the presentation of an order and movement that has all of the attributes of a formal processional but either parodies (as in Mardi Gras) or confronts (as in the Civil Rights Movement). For marchers with King the inversion occurred the moment African Americans entered public space where they had heretofore been deemed invisible. Not only were de jure and de facto prohibitions that separated the races tumbling down during each multiracial procession, but the sudden eruption of black presence into public space as peaceful contemplative activists shattered the social order's demonically constructed images of indolent black buffoons and criminals. This order relied upon consistent replication of negative images of Africana people to maintain segregation. The antidote to this ethereal poison was *presence*, peaceful sacrifice and unrelenting resolve.

The end result was that a purportedly Christian nation was forced to view its black citizens as a prototype of the Suffering God, absorbing violence into their own bodies without retaliation. By contrast stalwart defenders of the old order found themselves before God and their own reflective interiority with fire hoses, whips, and ropes in their hands. The crisis created by contemplative justice-seeking guaranteed the eventual end of overt practices of domination, for domination could not withstand the steady gaze of the inner eye of thousands of awakened people.

Grimes's theory of ritual provides an interesting lens to view the contemplative practices of the African American community but does not work as well to explicate the struggles of other Africana communities. Grimes contends that when dance and music are added to processions, they become a parade. He argues that "when dancing shifts from circularity and symmetry to linearity and asymmetry, the religious climate is likely to shift from prophetic criticism to priestly conservatism."[9] Although this may be true among certain dominant cultures and religions, it has less credence among people who value music and dance as an opportunity to mediate social conflict or to provide conduits to the transcendent. An excellent example can be found in South Africa. As the young people began to engage the power of the state and its apartheid policies, they would often dance throughout the night in tight circles that would unwind and process. The drums and rhythmic shouts and songs embodied the very essences of defiance and prophetic critique. The key for Grimes seems to be whether the processants are deemed to be integral to the dominant order. When they are not, they are free within the liminal space of their social isolation to choose their methods of communal expression.

The contemplative locus of the movement should not come as a surprise to those who survived the twentieth century. The crucial spiritual engagements were spun like a luminous web from the worn pews of black churches, tin shacks in South Africa, and American Indian reservations. Shouts, prayers and shut-ins, ritual enactments of the elders and ancestors prepared the way so that when Harriet Tubman headed into the thickets and Rosa settled into her seat, there was a contemplative faith history ready to accompany their acts of justice-seeking and activism.

A New View of Community

The turning point for North America was its acceptance of the moral lynchpin upon which the movement staked its claims. In the stillness that infused the hush arbors and prayer meetings a vision of justice emerged that could not be legislated. It emanated from divine interiority. Those marching merely reflected this reality. The mark of a Spirit-informed movement is incongruity. The sheer power of the systems of oppression looms impenetrably just before they crumble in seemingly inexplicable ways. Will prayerful marching around Jericho actually cause the walls to tumble? "Well, maybe," comes the unconvinced reply. These are natural events. If a system is corrupt and corroded from the inside out, then any shaking will cause it to fall. Believers and skeptics find common ground in this assertion. Yet the mark of dominant orders is their expert ability to hide the rot and internal decay, so that those who act in opposition find themselves facing the illusion of an impenetrable behemoth.

Who could have predicted that America's apartheid would fall as decisively as the walls of Jericho, when the people marched around the bastions of power carrying little more than their faith and resolve? How audacious it is to take what is given—the remnants of a chattel community, the vague memories of mother Africa, and a desperate need to be free—and translate those wisps into a multicultural, multivalent liberative vision of community. The idea of a beloved community emerged from the deeply contemplative activities of a besieged people. My own participation in these activities is crucial to my understanding of civil rights activism as contemplative.

Come before Winter

New Haven, the city of my upbringing, is a wintry place, a city of demand and debate. Although there are probably colder places, I am always reminded of Paul's entreaty "come before winter." The urgency to get things done in such places is palpable. This town nestled by the sea was the site of Amistad refuge and Panther trials. After relocating here, my family joined a socially activist and upwardly mobile African American Congregational church. Although the church eventually became affiliated with the United Church of Christ, its most memorable affiliation was with the Underground Railroad and hiding stations in its basement. In the lower levels of the church, dank and mysterious spaces still held their secrets. As children we sometimes thought that if you listened hard enough, you could almost hear the sounds of feet "runnin' for free."

This spiritual way station, which sat in the shadows of Yale University and the Winchester gun factory, evoked the danger, irony, and earnestness of a people on the move. Critical elements of faith, justice, and struggle seemed to coalesce in New Haven, Connecticut. Our church participated in the civil rights struggles and at the same time tried like crazy to be model citizens of a republic that resoundingly and smugly resisted those yearnings.

I grew up in the midst of these complexities. From the church's pews I went to Selma to march with King and then returned to have my church-affiliated debutante ball. The messages were conflicting: resist and succeed. But how does one resist the systems that must be appeased to allow those successes? The church that nurtured me also confused me. We were being mentored and guided toward a life considered to be black middle-class. Although we did not realize it at the time, this generational class leap would take all of our intellectual and emotional efforts.

Yet there was the call to connect to the struggle of the community. Since I had not yet heard of the scientific theory of complementarity—the ability to hold diametrically opposed ideas or realities within the same conceptual microcosm—my friends and I considered material success and social consciousness to be alternatives that would lead in completely divergent directions. Most of us began to move toward the possibility of individual success rather than communal well-being. This was not a rejection of the community but rather a commissioning. We would be explorers in the white world. We would be educated, and then when we had achieved our goals, we would uplift the race.

How could we know that while the Civil Rights Movement was gaining strength, the strengths of the black community were being dissipated? It was a silent revolution of sorts. This was a revolution supported by particular rites of passage that were deeply ensconced within the social structures of the black community. Often these rites had implicit contemplative overtones. The black communities in North America during the twentieth century were betwixt and between realities and meaning structures.[10] They were clothed in the invisibility that accrued to them as a result of race, yet they were fully invested with humanity as a result of self-realization within the context of family and faith.

The black church was a safe harbor and a spiritual refuge. In fact, during the years of slavery and oppression it had become a taken-for-granted necessity. Now the yearning within the community was for individual achievement and competitive feats. To enter this race toward equality meant turning away from communal values. It also required that we forget the ancestral legacies that had sustained us. Notwithstanding double standards with regard to gender and sexuality, most were committed across class lines to the wholeness and protection of the entire community. The movement toward diversification of this closed system was inevitable as social constraints eased, but we had no regrets since we believed with all of our hearts that the community would be there if and when we ever returned. We were wrong.

It is not easy to find that locus of spiritual support anymore. It has slipped from view. In just one generation, those who had the means to leave have become economic and cultural exiles. Even those who were left behind are not the same. It is nearly impossible to recognize the historical antecedents to "thug life" in the hopes of the community that preceded them. Certainly, the widespread focus on immediate gratification and materialism is confounding for a people who made survival an art form.

We began this one-way journey toward "integration" by identifying with the dominant culture and mimicking its rituals and lifestyles. Legal barriers fell so quickly that there was no time to authenticate our choices, to anchor them securely to the cultural flagship of Africana faith and practice. During the sprint toward equality, however, certain perspectives surfaced in ways that allowed the community to hold contradictory beliefs and ideas in dialectical tension without collapsing options into one category or another. My debutante ball was a prime example.

Marching for Freedom:
Waltzing with Upward Mobility

Although in retrospect it seems painfully incongruous to have a pre-teen debutante ball in an era of Panther trials, Malcolm X's emergence, and the escalating Civil Rights Movement in the South, this is exactly what we did. But before the curtsy came the march. Soon after the four little girls were killed in the church bombing in Alabama, our church, Dixwell Avenue Congregational, prepared to send a group of teens and adults South to participate in the marches. We would go into small towns to support civil rights workers who were risking their lives every day.[11]

After the big march in Selma we returned to prepare for our "social debut." In many ways the ball was an inversion ritual that challenged the status quo, because African American girls in my community were preparing to bow into a society that considered us to be invisible. We were teens searching for identity amid the blurred events of a nonviolent revolution and practiced curtsies. One thing was certain: our days of invisibility were numbered when we declared our "beingness" in a white dress with a hoop skirt. Long before James Brown sang "I'm Black and I'm Proud," club women and church ushers decided that their children would defy Jim Crow and dance with that old black magic, self-esteem. Faced with daunting personal and communal challenges, we affirmed the *imago dei* in dark-skinned, broken, gay, and feminine bodies.

The civil rights marches and debutante ball were rites of passage that seemed completely unrelated. I wanted the dots connected for me; instead, we were given experiential puzzle pieces to decipher and situate in our individual and communal lives. Such initiation rites inevitably draw the initiate inward, as this is the only site of potential resolution. And so, after developing contemplative practices on our front porches and on well-worn pews, we marched for freedom and waltzed into a society that rejected us.

Confusion was inevitable. Although there were probably myriad reasons for the confusion, one cause seems evident: the development of an interior life was also associated with assimilation, gentility, and upward mobility. Further confusion resulted because the community that needed us to bring our youth and energy to the enhancement of the common good also encouraged us to make great leaps toward materialistic successes. As pioneers on integration's frontier, we had to trade memories of our days as elementary-school anchorites and social revolutionaries for "cross-over careers" that would catapult us into the "white world." The stillness that had evolved on the porch was translated into career moves and civil practices that would create cataclysmic cultural changes.

Like the iceman who delivered ice to my great-grandmother in the 1930s and '40s, I bear phantom traces of all that has gone before. I have been told stories about the iceman, who would use sharp tongs to pick up a block of ice. If he miscalculated, that piece would bear the marks of the tongs, sharp, deeply carved, and temporary. Grandma Booker would often say that once the ice melted, you could no longer see the marks, but you remembered where they had been. "Life is just like that," she would conclude. Assimilation tactics subliminal and overt are like the tong-scarred ice. The community would be with you whether you wanted it to or not. Its invisible imprint lasted long after your exodus.

This transformative idea of community far exceeded the dream language that cloaked it. Instead, its contours could be described more accurately as a fully clothed prophetic vision that emerged from the yearning of the people. It was such a hopeful time. With the constraints of segregation loosened, those who had faithfully prayed for deliverance believed that the community would emerge as inevitably as an iceberg on the Arctic horizon. We assumed that all goals would be reached in progressive and linear increments. Instead we were faced with cycles of accomplishment and defeat. Rabbi Arthur Waskow retrospectively recognizes the cycles of oppression that justice-loving people experience: "In every generation there will be a pharaoh that rises to oppress us."[12]

No one could have predicted that the same community that marched and sat in together would begin to kill one another for sneakers, territory, and drugs. The new pharaohs arose as internalized task masters in the guise of nihilism and self-hatred. No one could have predicted that the studding of black males enforced during slavery would be voluntarily assumed by postmodern black men who now sire but will not father, mothers who bear but will not suckle, down-low brothers who secretly engage in sporadic high-risk same-sex liaisons while maintaining macho love matches with unsuspecting women, homophobia in the churches, and a deafening ecclesial silence in response to the devastation of AIDS.

Some attribute these self-destructive acts to conspiracy, the purposeful targeting of ethnic communities for drugs and dissolution. That is an allegation I can neither confirm nor deny. However, I can ask the question, Where is the moral resolve that kept the justice movements on the path toward fruition without money, without resources, with only a community beloved and contemplated? To reclaim we must once again pause and consider the contours of this community. Do we still have the same goals? Do King's words still ring true? Where is the community-called-beloved when we need it most?

Henri Nouwen describes the essence of community from a spiritual perspective. He says, "the basis of the Christian community is not the family or social or economic equality, or shared oppression or complaint, or mutual attraction . . . but the divine call."[13] This is an important aspect of community that is overlooked. According to Nouwen, the Christian community is a waiting community.[14] But it is also a group of people who pray the reality of their sense of belonging into being.

In recent years, many of us bemoan the failure of the beloved community to materialize in an objective way. It seems to be stuck in a time warp, tangled up in dream language and unrealistic expectations of reconciliation without repentance. False reconciliations expect victims of oppression to forget, absolve, and move on without acknowledgment of misdeeds or repentance, and for oppressors to apologize but keep the spoils of unmerited privilege. This is not the type of reconciliation that King recommended. When King painted a picture of the ultimate goals of the community called beloved, he necessarily—for reasons of time and rhetorical impact—omitted the tedious steps and sacrifices that would pave the way for its emergence.

But the most hidden aspect of community formation was the necessity of intentional contemplative practices as a spiritual precursor to the participation of a co-creating God. Nouwen makes the connection clear. It is through rituals of silence, word, song, and gesture that we indicate our readiness for the indwelling of God. It is through the sacred space that emerges in the black church during abiding times, which may or may not be silent, that the contours of community become visible.

Public Mystics: Letting the Light Shine

There are always those who lead by example, who slash through the thick brush to prepare a path, whose prayers are remembered, and whose deeds live long after they have became ancestors. The people that I have selected as contemplatives in this chapter are exemplary. Some are known for their leadership or courage, but few are known for their contemplative contributions. I am seeking the ineffable in the ordinary, the mystical in the mundane, the transcendent in the midst of pragmatic justice-seeking acts. As a consequence the method of inquiry for this chapter shifts slightly from critical analysis to vignette.

The exemplars come from different eras, but most are from the twentieth century. The reader will recognize the names of Rosa Parks, Howard Thurman, Fannie Lou Hamer, and Martin Luther King Jr. Because much has been written about each of these figures, we think that we know all about them. Yet there are gaps even in the imaginative projections that purport to encapsulate their lives. What does it mean to be a public mystic, a leader whose interiority and communal reference points must intersect? How does one called to such monumental tasks traverse the landscape of public expectations and inner longing? The questions that inform this chapter focus on the nature of contemplation in the lives of well-known civil rights leaders.

To date, we have drawn their lives as completed images that comport with our retrospectives desires. However, to understand the contemplative aspects of their lives, we must sketch the details of their lives with a eye to spiritual realities. Howard Thurman wrote in a 1958 issue of *Bostonia* magazine of his attempts to draw a penguin. He said, "I make no attempt at a realistic picture of a penguin. . . . A friend of mine once gave me a book on penguin anatomy—it cramped my style. . . . When I do a 'creative phantasy' I'm imagining a penguin as a penguin sees himself. And no one can dispute my interpretation."[15] Thurman is said to have let the penguins grow out of the end of his brush. The following depictions grow out of the remarks of the subjects, their writings, and the brush of historical memory that paints us all.

Fannie Lou Hamer: The Sick and Tired "Saint"
What manner of woman was this? She had such a familiar face and figure that you expected to see her at your own family

reunion. The moment you set eyes on her you recognized her as a relative even if you knew that she was not. She had the visage of a laboring woman and a determination to match the presence. Although her body was familiar, it was not her own. The system of segregation could kill, beat, or disfigure her at will. The assault upon her humanity was complete when she was subjected to one of the first involuntary hysterectomies (also known as a "Mississippi appendectomy") inflicted on poor rural women in the South.[16]

She was born on October 6, 1917, in the violent and oppressive county of Montgomery, Mississippi, and grew up in a loving but poverty-stricken sharecropping family. Rosetta Ross in her excellent account of black women in the Civil Rights Movement quotes Hamer on the issue of work in Mississippi: "We worked all the time . . . just worked and then we would be hungry and my mother was clearing up a new ground trying to help feed us for $1.25 a day. She was using an axe, just like a man."[17] While wielding the axe, Hamer's mother lost an eye. It seems that one hardship followed upon another, and Hamer and her family were trapped in a system of indentured labor.

I have chosen her as a contemplative exemplar because of her spiritual focus and resolve. Her practices spoke to the depth of her contemplative spirit. In the face of catastrophic suffering, Hamer worked, loved, sang, and resisted the powers that be. She was jailed, beaten, and hunted by the enforcers of the social order after registering to vote. The treatment was so brutal that Andrew Young was sent to get her out of jail. Yet she was kind to jailers who had been beating her for a week.[18] Where do you go in your spirit and mind when someone is beating you mercilessly? What peace have you summoned to smile at the executioner?

I remember Fannie Lou Hamer as a figure of the Civil Rights Movement whose tenacity brought the Democratic Party to a temporary accountability and struck fear into the Republicans. All of this was not-so-distant history until I met one of her colleagues at a conference convened by Charles Marsh that focused on Lived Theology and Civil Courage. It was a unique gathering of academics and elders of the Movement, her friends and confidantes, and warriors of the Mississippi race wars.

For some reason still unknown to me, I could not pay attention to the plenary address given by Victoria Gray Adams. She is a regal woman, a friend of Hamer, and an activist in her own right. Her address began carefully. Her speech was measured; the cadence was slow. She had lived so many decades in a struggle for respectability that now in front of these serious scholars of all things religious, she was determined not to stumble or misspeak. Her caretaking lulled me into a reverie. I would like to say that I entered a contemplative space, but I think that I fell asleep. I deeply regretted this lapse. How often do you get to hear Fannie Lou Hamer's contemporary speak about her life and the Movement to which all of us had dedicated our lives?

In the evening, when the stress of the day was over, I sat with Hamer's husband as he talked of hurried clandestine meetings, fear, and courage in the face of insurmountable odds. He mentioned the calm that always preceded the storm and the sense of destiny that did not need words to empower it. They were in this together, come what may. When Adams joined us, I asked my stupid question: "Why did Fannie Lou Hamer die so young?" The answer seems obvious to those who know that Hamer died from the ravages of diabetes, cancer, hypertension, and the lack of medical care in the richest country in the world. Adams looked at me with a mix of weariness and patience. "Don't you get it?" she said. "If it hadn't been for the Civil Rights Movement she would have died sooner." No, I didn't get it. So I persisted: "She had serious medical conditions, but what does that have to do with the Movement?" The griot emerged in Mrs. Adams as she settled herself down on a bench in the fancy museum where the gathering was being held. She placed her hand over mine and said, "She picked cotton. Do you know what that means?" She was kind; she did not even wince at the naiveté of this dislocated Yankee. Instead, she continued: "She was worn out from heat, and cotton, and trying to raise her children in a black-child-killin' place."[19]

It had never occurred to me that the Civil Rights Movement could become a monastic space, an opportunity for respite for a woman who had been " 'buked and scorned" by the black-woman/man/child-killing system of the day. Even in her beatings there was peace, because at least the forces of evil were being dragged into the light of day with every blow. I realize that there may be abused persons who will misinterpret my meaning. Options and responses to abuse differ from situation to situation; however, there is never a time when I would lift up submission to abuse as a model response. Nevertheless, when the system wields its life-crushing power, counterintuitive responses often yield the most fruitful results. Hamer was centered; she drew power from the example of her parents in their struggle to transcend the impossible situation of their lives. She faced daunting odds, as she was not dealing with an abusive individual but instead the power of federal, state, and local governments and cultural traditions that deemed her to be a nonperson. This designation of nonper-sonhood did not deter her, for her contemplative entry into a deeper "knowing" came through her commitment to nonviolence.

Adherence to the spiritual disciplines of civil rights activism required that she love the crucifier, bless the torturer, embrace the jailer, and pray for his or her salvation. She did this and more. This description of Hamer's piety and commitment brings me to a stopping point. I am not one who relishes the glorification of good deeds in the lives of individuals. I shy away from the report-ing of laudatory exploits, because as an ethicist I believe that goodness is our ordinary task, that it is the sinew between soul and spirit strengthened by the choice to do what is fitting and right. Yet the example that Hamer sets requires recognition.

According to her friend Virginia Gray Adams, "her back hurt and her spirit waged war without proper food or medicine. So when the Movement came, there was rest"—not the rest that pervades the lives of most contemplatives, but rest nonetheless. Rest as you tell Congress to let your people go. Rest as you tes-tify and lead a delegation off the floor of the Democratic Con-vention. Rest comes as rest comes—sometimes in the great feather beds of the wealthy and sometimes just a step away from hard labor. When it comes, it is balm to the spirit and solace to the soul. This is a rest that wafts from a wellspring of intentional justice-seeking as spiritual practice. These practices allow one to live in and out of the body and to inhabit hope as an ethereal but more permanent enfleshment. Fannie Lou Hamer was cloistered in an activist movement, finding her focus, restoration, and life in God in the midst of the beloved community already here and yet coming.

And so on April 14, 1977, the plain-talking, hard-working saint from Mississippi, an unlikely prophet who was "sick and tired of being sick and tired," died at the age of fifty-nine. In his eulogy Andrew Young said, "She literally, along with many of you, shook the foundations of this nation. . . . Mrs. Hamer was special, but she was also representative. Hundreds of women spoke up and . . . learned the lessons that inspired the women's movement."[20] The story ends here, but it is the beginning of stories that will be told wherever justice-loving people gather. Once upon a time there was a contemplative mother, a brave and wise woman of few words who entered the Civil Rights Movement as a novitiate enters a convent—not for retreat but for the restorative love of the community and the space to fight for justice. She spoke when speaking was necessary and led always by example, letting her little light shine.

Martin Luther King Jr.: Riding a Spiritual Tidal Wave

A positive religious faith does not offer an illusion that we shall be exempt from pain and suffering, nor does it imbue us with the idea that life is a drama of unalloyed comfort and untroubled ease. Rather, it instills us with the inner equilibrium needed to face strains, burdens, and fears that inevitably come, and assures us that the universe is trustworthy and God is concerned.[21]

So much has been written about King, and yet it seems that he becomes more and more opaque as time goes on. This may be because we project upon this great spiritual leader our retrospective critiques and expectations. I think of King as a great contemplative, one who used the spiritual essence of nonviolence as a tool for liberating the social order and the spiritual authority of a denigrated people. The power of the contemplative life becomes evident as we watch a man steeped in the hierarchical and rather static and entrenched ecclesial systems of denominational church life change direction. King's intention when he returned to the South was to take his comfortable and prepared place in that long line of preachers in his family; however, it was not to be.

As events unfolded, it often seemed that King was running behind the movement, representing it, speaking on its behalf, but allowing its life to come from the people who were putting their lives on the line. Truth be told, it was not the black church in its static and familiar denominational guise, but the meta-actual church embodied in the resolve of young people that caught the vision of the visionary. Although their energy was mediated through the discourses and systems of the church, the Movement was not ignited by the progressive inevitability of church planning.

The church did not understand what was going on until the movement was well underway. As Jesse Jackson notes, it is only in retrospect that the black church has fully embraced King and a revisionist version of his life and beliefs.[22] They are still not comfortable with the King who rejected capitalism and used anti-war rhetoric. King is blurred and co-opted in our postmodern appropriations because we have assigned him to a static identity and ironed out the contradictions that are often found in the lives of contemplatives.

The specific characteristics that point to the contemplative aspects of King's life include: authenticity that did not emanate from inherited respectability; spiritual transience that allowed him to follow the impetus of the communal and divine will rather than imposing a direction; and awareness of the rhythms of deliverance, coming in and out of exile. Speaking with an authentic voice in an age of formal oration is not easy. King was a preacher, but his public voice exceeded the boundaries of homiletical prowess. Instead, he used his voice to amplify the voices of the voiceless. When you hear him or read his speeches, you hear not only the rhythms of black Baptist oratory and the utterances of a living prophet but also the voice of the community. He spoke as a human megaphone, articulating commonly held beliefs as if the community spoke in unison through him. His words echoed in all hearts, even in those of his opponents.

Spiritual transience is the story of biblical call. Inevitably you find yourself in places you never expected to be. The willingness to wander at the bidding of the Spirit is settled long before the journeys begin. It is settled during prayer and contemplation when desires and self-direction give way in favor of spiritual leading. King found himself in situations that reason would not choose, witnessing where politically astute leaders would fear to tread. Before racism was dead, his talk turned to the necessity of an anti-war stance; before the South had relented, he was demonstrating in the North and facing the intractable systems of those who hide their racial disdain behind their liberal acts. He seemed to be following and listening, adjusting for the moment-by-moment changes that occurred as he journeyed with a community on the move.

Finally, King recognized the rhythms that prevail when you are coming in and out of exile. There are no linear paths when you follow the contemplative way. Escaping one set of circumstances usually invites another set. If you are coming out of Egypt, you are going into the wilderness, emerging from segregation and entering the exilic event of legally imposed integration. In the realm of the Spirit stationary goals are mythologies that obscure intersecting realities. The signposts that mark progress are internal as well as external. The indicator of King's purposes and progress came from his implementation of agape love.

King defined agape as "the love of God operating in the human heart."[23] The journey toward complete dependence on God culminated with his famous "I See the Promised Land" speech. The metaphorical language that King used hints at an inward journey. Surrounded by threatening situations, he had prayed through and had seen with his spiritual eye both the Promised Land and the coming of the Lord. Like Moses, he had seen but would not inhabit. The reasons are God's.

The parallel to Moses seems obvious, but there are also spiritual intersections with the prophet Anna. She was allowed to see Jesus before she died. Although she would not be around for the sermons, miracles, or acts of deliverance, her sight was sufficient—sufficient because she saw not just with natural eyes but also with the spiritual and contemplative depth that allows God's Spirit to respond to the pleas of the heart. On the night before King's death, we all saw the face of a man who had been in the presence of the holy and who feared nothing. As a consequence, the shot that fulfilled his prophecy was horrendous but also anticlimactic.

King had just the night before reassured us that the person or motive responsible for dispatching his human body was of little concern. King had already relinquished his life to God on the mountaintop. But where was that mountain? I live in Memphis, a city that has not forgiven itself for being the site of King's death. I can tell you that there are no mountains—a few hills, but no crests of rock that touch the clouds. So King's spiritual mountaintop is a very interesting metaphoric choice.

I believe that his use of this phrase was a hint about his own contemplative journey. Perhaps the steepest climb on the life journey is toward death. It requires trust that may not have developed during life; it requires relinquishment of attachments. It is an arduous task. When Jesus sweats in Gethsemane, he is also mountain climbing, relinquishing and accepting. At the top of this mountain of obedience and necessity King communed with God and was offered freedom in ways that he had never imagined.

During this theophany God's intent was revealed to him like a film preview, giving King the impetus to say, "I've looked over. And I've seen the Promised Land. I may not get there with you. But I want you to know tonight, that we as a people will get to the Promised Land. And I'm happy tonight. I'm not worried about anything. I'm not fearing any man. Mine eyes have seen the glory of the coming of the Lord."[24] King's contemplative turn toward the source of all being gave him peace. He was at the right place during the right time in history, when God's deliverance rolled down like water through the bastions of injustice.

Rosa Parks: Contemplation and Lay Activism

> I had no idea that history was being made. I was just tired of giving in. Somehow, I felt that what I did was right by standing up to that bus driver. I did not think about the consequences. I knew that I could have been lynched, manhandled, or beaten when the police came. I chose not to move. When I made that decision, I knew that I had the strength of the ancestors with me.[25]

Any anchorite worth her salt seals herself up in a church and dedicates her life to the worship of God, but a bus, a cell on wheels— can this really be a space of respite and revolution? In the tradition of those who sacrifice with prayer and dedication, Rosa Parks prepared herself spiritually and practically for the tasks to come. Her ten days at Highlander Folk School[26] began the healing process within. She noted that during her brief stay she interacted with whites as equals and extinguished some of the anger and resentment she had internalized. Although she attended the Highlander meetings in preparation for nonviolent initiatives, nothing could have prepared her for the events of that day.

Some say that she was a "professional" resister—maybe, maybe not. Battered self-respect and weary feet are equally sound motivations for refusing to leave a bus seat when challenged. But this is all in retrospect. At the time of her resistance nothing was certain. The news story very well could have been: "A middle-aged black woman was killed in a bus incident today after her refusal to obey the laws of segregation." At the moment that you stare into the fires stoked by oppression, seven times their usual heat, you cannot know that one "like the son of God" will be with you—all you can see is fire. Yet she sat. While people yelled at her and the police threatened, she sat. The stillness within became a sign of external dignity and a model of contemplative activism.

When she was asked to vacate her seat, three other black passengers were also asked to move from a row of seats behind the whites-only section. They obeyed; she did not. As a lay woman acquainted with the struggle for justice, her actions become the quintessential expression of the power of the laity. Mediated through her stance is the witness of those who had gone before her. Contemplation ensconced in a reflective and spiritually alert laity was the foundation for the success of this Movement and many others.

Rosa Parks's story is important because she emerged during the Civil Rights Movement as a catalyst for change. Her act of civil disobedience became one of the important rallying events of the Movement. What could be more contemplative then the act of sitting silently? No matter that she spent ten days at Highlander. No matter that her middle-class upbringing was necessary to forestall the moral criticism used as a cover to indict protesters. In silence, in peace she sat.

A successful movement had to begin in exactly this way, led by a lay person whose ordinary life was known by all in the community. She could be trusted. Who knew where the leaders were getting their power? They were in the position to broker deals, to negotiate with both sides of an issue, and even to be compensated for taking a particular stance in volatile community situations. Through this lay woman a community of Africans in the Americas heard the drumbeat of inevitability and sat down all over the South. At lunch counters and segregated church services they sat. They were not all in one place, but they sat together as the blows of the institutions of segregation rained on their heads.

"At the jailhouse, Parks asked if she could have a drink from the water fountain and was told it was for whites only. She then was fingerprinted, booked, and put in a cell with two other black women, one of whom gave her a drink of water from a dark metal mug."[27] Cool waters that refresh the soul can come from waters in a dark metal mug. Who would not prefer a spring or fresh-flowing river? But when those sources have been co-opted or removed from your reach, water from a mug in a friend's hand is a blessed offering. Once in a generation there is a Thérèse of

Leiseux, a Sojourner Truth, a Fannie Lou Hamer whose refusal to succumb becomes the center of the movement toward justice. Like Queen Esther, Rosa Parks emerges at such a time as this to embody not just nonviolence but also the contemplative strength of the laity empowered by God's justice and the wisdom of the gathered community.

Sue Bailey and Howard Thurman:
Listen for the Sound of the Genuine Within

The Thurmans are trailblazers in the arena of contemplative and mystical studies. Because much has been written about their lives, this vignette seeks only insight into their public mysticism. Although there were many exemplars with spiritual depth in Africana traditions, few claimed those gifts as the center of their religious thought. Howard Thurman did just that. Biographers imply that he had spiritual inclinations from the beginning, having been born "with the veil" in segregated Daytona, Florida. In the black folk tradition, children born with the veil have second sight and can interpret and connect to the spirit realm. All types of remedies for this "condition" were available. In Thurman's case, his ears were pierced to "dissipate clairvoyance."

As far as Thurman is concerned, deep spirituality is not just the result of birthright and folk interpretations; he is also highly cognizant of his place in a broader universe. In *With Head and Heart*, Thurman recalls seeing Halley's Comet and feeling connected to something more profound than the petty social arrangements that relegated him to the margins of society.[28] But public mysticism was an unusual choice for black people in Thurman's day. It seemed to be a most impractical pursuit. People wanted normalcy, safety, and opportunity. They heard the elders talk of mystery but relegated those discussions to the private realm. Yet Thurman could not conceive of life without the mystical. His creativity allowed him to translate his sense of centeredness into artful worship services that celebrated ritual and drama.

In 1935 he and his wife, Sue Bailey Thurman, went to India, Burma, and Ceylon. During this trip they met Mohandas Gandhi and talked with him about the issues of persecution. Sue Bailey was a fascinating woman.[29] Along with her work with Thurman in the development of the first interracial, nondenominational church in the United States, she was also an activist who worked tirelessly for women's causes and for the ultimate equal rights of all. Richard Newman describes their work as pilgrimage from the clear-cut context of the black church to an unknowing reunion with all humankind and the divine.

Walter Fluker, a Thurman scholar and one who knew him and worked with him, discusses a moment of angst in 1980 when he asked Thurman for career advice: "Thurman wrote back, 'You must wait and listen for the sound of the genuine that is within. When you hear it, it will be your voice and that will be the voice of God.'"[30] I can sense the alarm of the literalist, who considers the unity of voices divine and human to be blasphemous. However, Thurman's recognition that there is no separateness of person, space, or religious inclination (despite our need to categorize) is his particular contemplative gift. Thurman reaches beyond the familiar to embrace the possible:

> There is a spirit abroad in life of which the Judaeo-Christian ethic is but one expression. It is a spirit that makes for wholeness and for community. . . . It broods over the demonstrators for justice and brings comfort to the desolate and forgotten who have no memory of what it is to feel the rhythm of belonging. . . . It knows no country and its allies are to be found wherever the heart is kind and the collective will and the private endeavor seek to make justice where injustice abounds.[31]

In Thurman's time his interfaith initiatives were groundbreaking; the reflective gaze of history confirms that his prescience was a precursor to our current global community. He and Sue Bailey understood the exigencies of the day and the focus of other spiritual leaders on the needs of besieged Africana communities, but they also realized that when you "center down" you may be called to exceed the boundaries of your own community and its needs to embrace your neighbors. Their spiritual witness is that God "so loves the world" with all of its variant faith expressions and that God's spirit broods over us and sustains us without regard to national or religious boundaries—requiring of us not liturgical conformity but justice, peace, and kind hearts.

Malcolm X (El Hajj Malik El Shabazz)

Like Augustine, Malcolm X was a contemplative whose life was layered and enriched by multiple conversion experiences. He was born Malcolm Little in 1925. When he died, he was known as El Hajj Malik El Shabazz and better known as Malcolm X. His life was deeply affected by racism and violence at an early age. When he was a young boy, his father, a Baptist preacher and organizer with Marcus Garvey's Back to Africa movement, was murdered by white dissidents. Malcolm noted that his mother had a premonition of the murder and tried to call her husband back to the house as he headed for town.[32] Malcolm claimed to have the same empathic ability.

The death of his father changed their financial circumstances drastically and precipitated their move north to stay with relatives. There Malcolm drifted into criminal behavior. His autobiography describes the onslaughts of a racist society and his increasingly resistant response to it. He was arrested in 1946 and served a seven-year sentence. It was during his prison term that Malcolm's first conversion experience occurred, and he became aware of the contemplative aspects of his spiritual life. bell hooks offers a unique glimpse of the contemplative Malcolm in confinement:

> Confinement in prison provides the space where Malcolm can engage in uninterrupted critical reflection on his life, where he can contemplate the meaning and significance of human existence. During this period of confinement, he comes face to face with the emptiness of his life, the nihilism. This time for him is akin to "a dark night of the soul." . . . He is overwhelmed with longing, without knowing for what he longs. It is in that space of need that he is offered Islam.[33]

He accepted this lifeline and became deeply committed to the Nation of Islam. His devotion to Elijah Muhammad and his years of celibacy prior to his marriage to Betty Shabazz were elements of his deeply contemplative inclinations. Of this aspect of his life bell hooks says, "Taking a vow of celibacy was one of the ways Malcolm expressed this devotion. He sought no personal love relationships because he felt they would interfere with his spiritual quest, with his commitment to serve his master."[34] His own description of the matter-of-fact precursors to his marriage gives us hints of this pragmatic aspect of his personality. Clearly, Malcolm mediated his contemplative disposition through an intense engagement with the world and its issues.

For many Christians the word *contemplation* is synonymous with their own specifically Christian belief system. Accordingly it is difficult to situate Malcolm's contemplative spirit. Michael Eric Dyson notes the differences between Malcolm's spirituality and the spirituality of the black church in his discussion of Spike Lee's 1992 film about Malcolm's life. He says:

> The markers of black spirituality have been dominated by the Christian cosmos; the themes, images, and ideas of black spiritual life are usually evoked by gospel choirs enthralled in joyous praise or a passionate preacher engaged in ecstatic proclamation. Never before in American cinema has an alternative black spirituality been so intelligently presented.[35]

Malcolm evidenced a quiet authority that drew its strength from the rhetoric of political empowerment and a focused spiritual intent. Malcolm's devotion to Elijah Muhammad was contingent upon the integrity of Elijah's leadership. His moral intensity was not based on ethical formulas or rules; rather it emanated from a deeply resonant inner reality. As Elijah Muhammad's moral failures became apparent and Malcolm's public power soared, the relationship ended and Malcolm had another conversion experience.

When I use the word *conversion* I am not implying any judgment as to the veracity or context for these shifts of religious orientation. Some scholars problematize the "convenience" of his last conversion. I do not think it matters; what is more important is Malcolm's willingness to journey, even when the path requires a rejection of formerly dearly held values. And so he embraces classical Islamic teachings and journeys to Mecca. During this entire period Malcolm's life is mediated through passionate oratory and critical thinking. There is never a moment when people in his presence feel swept away by the depth of his other-worldliness. Instead, he is grounded in a contemplative tradition that expects a practical translation of the spiritual into accessible resources for the community.

Like King, Malcolm is bigger than life and subject to our romanticized suppositions. Yet his contemplative spirit is a call to the Africana community to recognize the sources of their own oppression, including their complicity in its perpetuation. He often used the language of waking up the "Negro," waking up the nation. Although Malcolm disavowed his "white devil" language after Mecca, it is clear that contemplation did not draw him away from the community. Instead, he became a lightning rod in its midst, impassively drawing the wrath of the dominant culture and those who desperately wanted to assimilate. In his final years he proposed a dramatic shift from civil to human rights. This is a movement that we are still trying to bring to fruition.

Some followers believe that it was his connection to the wider Islamic and African nations and his attestation that North American blacks should seek help from and reconnect with the global community that set the assassination in motion. Malcolm knew as he entered the Aurora ballroom that the Nation of Islam did not have the power or reach to affect him in the ways that he was being affected in the last months of his life. In a flash of mystical insight he called his wife and had her dress and bring his four children to hear his last speech.

Almost fifty years later the mysteries abound. None of the currently living generations will be alive when the truth about the era of assassinations is finally told. Suffice it to say that Malcolm was killed when he broadened the liberation movement to mainstream Islam and the African nations, and Martin was killed when he broadened the Civil Rights Movement from lunch counter sit-ins to a cross-cultural economic battle for the rights of the poor regardless of color.

Malcolm was a wide-eyed mystic—a man who had visions, embraced celibacy, married without fanfare as if he knew what few of us know, which partner would labor with him and bring her own gifts into his life. Although some scholars accuse him of manipulation in his successive conversions, particularly the final shift to Islam, I wonder if he had simply learned to embrace the faith that embraced him. When the object of your devotion is lost, when the goals that you thought were God-given fail, you have a choice to remain where you are, despondent and bereft, or you may follow the dimly lit path toward greater wisdom. Malcolm and Martin always chose the latter option.

Once-in-a-Lifetime Blooms

According to a romantic myth, the century plant, also known as the Mexican Tree of Life and Abundance or *agave deserti*, blooms only once in its lifetime. In fact, botanists say that it blooms every twenty to thirty years, but once it blooms, it dies. It uses all of its energy to produce the sprouts for the next generation. The civil rights generation is quickly moving toward the history books and the realm of ancestors. Those of us who have lived during this era have shared a unique opportunity to witness the flowering of this rare bloom, the quest for liberation in nonviolent and contemplative ways. Like this "tree of life," which provides food, fodder, twine, soap, and roofing, we have only begun to claim the treasures of a century of activism and contemplative justice-seeking.

The contemplatives who led the movements differed significantly in their spiritual orientations, but each journeyed inward and then returned to the community to share the gifts of the spirit. The seeds for the continuance of the liberation movements were produced at great cost. We have an obligation to continue the struggle, but perhaps we are still too close to the movements to find our way to the next site of God's in-breaking justice. Perhaps the next location for change and restoration will be in the hearts of the willing.

7

At the Crossroads
Secular Reclamations
of the Contemplative Life

When there's something you don't understand, you have to go humbly to it. You don't go to school and sit down and say, "I know what you're getting ready to teach me." You sit there and you learn. You open your mind. You absorb. But you have to be quiet, you have to be still, to do all this.
—John Coltrane

We are told that Jesus hung out with publicans, tax collectors, and sinners. Perhaps during these sessions of music, laughter, and food fellowship, there were also sacred moments when the love of God and mutual care and concern became the focus of their time together. Contemplation is not confined to designated and institutional sacred spaces. God breaks into nightclubs and Billie Holiday's sultry torch songs; God tap dances with Bill Robinson and Savion Glover. And when Coltrane blew his horn, the angels paused to consider.

Some sacred spaces bear none of the expected characteristics. The fact that we prefer stained glass windows, pomp and circumstance, and pastor's appreciation celebrations has nothing to do with the sacred. It may seem as if the mysteries of divine-human reunion erupt in our lives, when in fact the otherness of spiritual abiding is integral to human interiority. On occasion we turn our attention to this abiding presence and are startled. But it was always there.

For convenience I have titled this chapter "Secular," but it is no such thing. Here I engage a different sacred frequency—an extension of pulpit and pew, and perhaps one of the few viable space left for the creative exposition of the contemplative. Artists learned in their churches about the pauses. They learned that there were things too full for human tongues, too alive for articulation. You can dance and rhyme and sing it; you almost reach it in the high notes; but joy unspeakable is experience and sojourn, it is the ineffable within our reach.

When you least expect it, during the most mundane daily tasks, a shift of focus occurs. This shift bends us toward the universe within—that cosmos of soul and spirit, bone and flesh, which constantly reaches toward divinity. Ecclesial organizations want to control access to this milieu but cannot. The only divisions between the sacred and the secular are in the minds of those who believe in and reinforce the split.

Teresa Reed agrees that there are no radical disjunctures between the sacred and the secular, no gaping secular ditch waiting to swallow the faithful. Rather, all things draw from the same wellspring of spiritual energy. This means that the sermonic and religious can be mediated through a saxophone just as effectively as through a pastor. As the community has changed, the needs and sounds of "holiness" have diversified. Freedom cracked the chrysalis of safety that had been tightly woven around a community under siege. Now people were leaving the places of bondage for the uncharted world of chosen relationships, upward mobility, and exposure to other faith tenets. According to Reed, "by the 1970s black secular music had become as much a venue for preaching as the traditional pulpit of the black church. Just as the religious expectations of blacks had come to place heavy emphasis on social and political concerns, the secular dimension of black culture had also evolved to include the preaching voices once confined to the black church."[1] How can this be? Is Reed implying that tapping feet and blues guitar strokes can evoke the contemplative moment and call the listener to a deeper understanding of inner and outer realities? I ask these questions with tongue in cheek to underscore the discomfort that the black church has expressed toward its offspring in the arts. The need to create impermeable boundaries between the sacred and the secular is not a legacy of Africana culture. Rather, it is a much more recent appropriation of western values and categories.

In western cultures we speak of sacred and secular as separate realms. This configuration of the life space is alien to Africana culture. Consequently, it is no wonder that the black church and the art forms it has spawned are inextricably linked. They are connected not only by rhythmic cross-pollinations but also by a legacy of spiritual consciousness that recognizes the power and sacred potential of the human spirit in every life context.

The task of separating the sacred and secular becomes much more difficult when the same people in the juke joints are on the deacon boards and the rappers are the children of the ushers. Historically, most efforts to wall off the doctrinal rightness and wrongness of particular practices failed. Instead, hearers of the gospel inculturated and improvised on the main themes so as to tune the message for their own hearing. Given Christianity's preferential option for the poor, the cross-pollination of jazz, blues, and tap with church music and practices could be considered the epitome of missional outreach and spiritual creativity.

It is in the world that God so loved that the Spirit does its leading. We expect the saints to get tapped for divine favor, but often it is the least likely who are called. Because of the continuing false divisions between the sacred and the secular, one hardly expects to hear the witness of a singer such as Teddy Pendergrass, who was called like Samuel three times in the night. Pendergrass was a young man when he heard a voice in the night calling his name on three separate occasions. Teddy checked with his mother each time; neither of them can ascertain the source of the voice. Finally it became clear to both of them that he was being called by God. As they were praying together, his mothers said, "Something wonderful has occurred. . . . You have heard the voice of the spirit and received your calling."[2] Eventually, Pendergrass realized that his call was not to the traditional pulpit but to a ministry of music that unites secular and sacred. He was to express his faith through his voice, not singing gospel songs necessarily but sharing the gift that has been given. In the following examples, contemplation emerges in blues, jazz, and tap, a mystery that permeates not just houses of faith but also the arts.

Contemplation in Musical Genres

The Blues Critique of Religion

"While the 'quite religious' had the opportunity to express their mythologies, theologies, and theodicies in their church music, the 'somewhat religious' expressed their cosmology and religious ponderings in the blues."[3] Teresa Reed traces the development of blues from its emergence in black church music through the northern migration. The world was changing rapidly for people once considered to be property. Now as fully free human beings in a less than welcoming society, they sought answers to age-old questions and a move from survival modalities to engaged spirituality. Reed argues that the blues provided a means of critiquing the black church. As she says, "religion in these texts is far more than a creative resource. It is also a subject of contemplation."[4]

When Reed uses the word *contemplation*, it is clear that she is referring to thoughtful reflection using the modality of musical critique. Like the familiar laments in the book of Psalms, blues artists forthrightly engaged the issues in life that the church would not discuss—such as sexuality, theodicy, and the unabated despair of the people. The lyrics were straightforward and sometimes raunchy, but they captured the life experiences of the listeners. While gospel music promised peace in the hereafter and the promise of God's presence, the blues became public theology, communal inquiry, and a critique of the church.

Public theology is the engagement of discourse in the public sphere about issues of faith. It begins with the expectation of an ongoing dialogue with others who may or may not agree with the initial premise. During the dialogical exchange, ideas are honed and shaped as information is added and deleted. If the blues are considered public theology, they certainly reflect the depth of religious training gleaned from the church. This knowledge is being tested in the context of free and uncharted lives. As for communal inquiry, lyrics often raise shared and unspoken problems that are deemed too intimate or too forthright for church consideration. Bluesman Peter Chatman ("Memphis Slim") sings about the need for two working adults in the household long before the women's liberation movement. "You Got to Help Me Some" is not a love song, even when he alludes to late-night snuggling—he is repeating his plea, "if I bring in one dollar you bring one too." Encounters with a skewed justice system inspired Blind Lemon Jefferson to sing "Hangman's Blues"; Ma Rainey sings about "Blues and Booze." Issues of alcoholism, family support, and incarceration were not the themes of the weekly sermon, unless it was to rail against sin. The blues gave these musicians an opportunity to sing their lived theology.

And finally, the critique of the church becomes evident as blues singers spin the scats and minor-key challenges to otherworldly theological responses to real life problems. Questions abound in the lyrics. Why is the preacher sleeping with the women in the congregation while the husbands are at work? What is happening to the money from the special collections? Why is God not alleviating the sorrows of an urban workforce, laboring in a new and more challenging industrial "slavery"? The critiques are often oblique and satirical. Although blues are deemed to be a musical lament, there is often a trickster quality to the lyrics. Jokes and punch lines take their place along with the wailed entreaties of the brokenhearted. Repetition allows the listener to apply his or her own situation to the song.

The contemplative moment comes as the cause of the blues is considered within the broader context of God's inexplicable absence or startling intervention. Under every stanza is the silent and unspoken question, "How long, oh Lord, how long will your people continue to suffer?" Suffering is no longer emerging from the crisis of the institution of slavery; it is coming from the angst of living with meager means and few skills to negotiate relationships. Although the words of blues songs became the focus of church opposition to "the Devil's music," the words did not become the portal to contemplation. Instead, instruments—not unlike the talking drum—called people to consider their condition.

No one thinks for one moment that when B. B. King begins to sing, he is saying all that there is to be said about the subject. In fact, there is a purposeful avoidance of didactic phrasing and expository stanzas in the blues song. One or two lines hold the portal open for listeners to mentally supply the rest. This is the contemplative turn. B. B. King calls his guitar "Lucille," a reference to the presence and life energy of the instrument. Lucille calls the gathered listeners to a hearing that includes the memories of times past and hope for the future. Smoky nightclubs and juke joints become the spaces for pragmatic contemplation that attends to the details of daily life and the potential for its enrichment and ultimate transcendence.

Improvisational Jazz Contemplations

"Improvisation is a pragmatic device for confronting the fact that life is felt to be a 'lowdown dirty shame.'"[5] Jazz is a way of being in the world, a willingness to break away from rhetorical comfort zones and language hierarchies. When you know that you are "between a rock and a hard place," then you must respond creatively to the situation. Jazz is the musical version of the communal response to displacement. This is not a black thing; all North Americans are displaced immigrants. However, the displacement of the African diaspora was sealed by skin color as a permanent social exile. Some amelioration of that exile has only now begun. The improvisations that became secular music are riffs on the sacred and bear that imprint.

Improvisation is at the heart of Christianity. William Dean describes episodic precursors to improvisation as part of the American story. First, Americans found themselves cut off from an "ancient and structured culture"; second, they relocated to a place without that history; and finally, they created a new story.[6]

I find similarities in the story of Africana assimilation. Cut off from the culture and legacy of the African continent, arriving on the shores of an infant nation, they had to create a new reality in the midst of oppression.

Dean recognizes that "black loss and displacement are far more thorough and the place prepared for the blacks far more daunting than for other immigrants."[7] For Africans in the Americas "far more daunting" fails to capture the reality. Absolutely everything was strange and ominous. Their response to this strangeness and danger is creativity, improvisation, and the counterintuitive layering of joy and lament.

The improvisational motif in jazz music refers to the spontaneous creation of melodic innovations that diverge and meld with the main tune. "Jazz improvisation combines the complementary themes of shared community values and idiosyncratic [individual] musical perspectives."[8] Every "I" in the hymns and spirituals is the individual contribution to the "we" of the community. When the contributions of the individual improvisations soar, the contemplative potential increases. For in the midst of unthinkable rhythmic and tonal combinations, we also hear the impossible being brought within our reach.

When Miles Davis blows the cacophony that can barely be contained by the word *song*, we come closest to the unimaginable, the potential of the future, and the source of our being. Yet jazz musicians will tell you that improvisation is risky business. They will also tell you, as Coltrane did, that sometimes they receive their inspiration from divine sources. When you listen to Coltrane, you hear pain and possibility. The old neighborhood and the folks we left behind emerge behind half-notes. The straining trumpet blasts away the illusion that our upward mobility will bring peace.

But while jazz challenges and prods us, it also takes us to church. In a tribute to the Rev. John Gensel, the late jazz ministry pastor of St. Peter's Lutheran Church in New York City, Martin E. Marty made this observation about the relationship between jazz and worship:

What is it with theologians and jazz? Especially, why appre-
ciate jazz in worship . . . when the market urges churches to
use soft rock, light metal, whispered rap and, most of all,
muffled praise songs that sound like soulless elevator
music? . . . It can't be because the origins of jazz are all that
pure. We get reminded daily that this is music born in
saloons and brothels and other low-life places.[9]

Marty concludes that the key to understanding links between
worship and jazz is subsumed in the word *awe*. This is an
emotion that is accessible to everyone. He says that "jazz can
erupt in joy." Joy infused with the riffs of awe tends to be
unspeakable.

Jazz, like blues, is rooted in Delta rhythms. Alain Locke, noted
African American philosopher, contended that "jazz evolved
from the lower Mississippi strain, which had the most deeply traditional blues forms."[10] He recognized the potential for jazz to
point beyond the stanzas toward "the courage and gift to impro-
vise and interpolate, and a canny sense for the total effect."[11]
Locke also recognized the layered elements of jazz and its
remarkable "cultural overtones."[12]

He also noted the importance of jazz in the life of the community. He realized that jazz "incorporated the typical American restlessness and unconventionality, embodied its revolt
against the drabness of commonplace life, put pagan force
behind the revolt against Puritan restraint, and finally became
the Western world's life-saving flight from boredom and over-
sophistication to the refuge of elemental emotion and primitive
vigor."[13] To reach the center of your own soul, sometimes you
must fly low under the main paradigm, to bring a fresh word to
a word-saturated culture.

Blues and hip hop work out their issues in the manner of the
griots. They weave their stories into verbal challenges and lan-
guorous love chants. The words of rhythmic prophecy and
lament spill into daily life in juke joints and on the streets. Language grapples with theodicy and aesthetics in blues and hip
hop. For tap and jazz, metered ineffability must suffice. Tap and

jazz provide unexplored but fertile ground to consider contemplative resources in the black community. As we have noted in previous chapters, Africana approaches to contemplation do not require silence but can flare in the midst of a shout or trumpet blast. As a consequence some of the most focused spiritual energy can be found in jazz and tap dancing.

Tap Dancing

There is a whole generation of folks who are uncomfortable with tap dancing. I had no sense of this discomfort until I was talking to a middle-aged man from southern Georgia. I was thrilled to be going to see *Bring in 'Da Noise, Bring in 'Da Funk*, a spectacular tap-dancing show that featured Savion Glover. The man's reaction was similar to the reaction that some have to slave artifacts: "Why do we have to remember these embarrassing aspects of our past?" Or, with regard to tap dancing: "This is what we did to entertain 'the white man' when we had no power. It's time to move on."

I was stunned. It never occurred to me that tap dancing would be anything but a joy for all to behold. After all, I was raised by a mother and father who defied poverty and danced at the Savoy ballroom in New York. They punctuated their segregated lives with the rebellious rhythms of Bill Robinson. Given such a rich aesthetic legacy, I wondered how anyone could feel intimidated or embarrassed by such immense talent. I presumed the reaction to be a holdover from the ambivalence that arose in black communities during the minstrel era when blackface and tap shoes provided amusement to the dominant culture.

I thought no more about it until I was at a conference in Oakland. Prior to a speech by Congresswoman Barbara Lee, a young Anglo woman tap danced the shame still attached to the art of tap dancing in a piece called "Don't Do It." She said and tapped what I had been hearing on the "down low." Once the Civil Rights Movement opened societal doors, those who were positioned to take advantage of the new opportunities did not want to be reminded of times past. For many who lived during the era of siege, tap dancing epitomized servility and accommodation. It took young talented tappers to return the art to its rightful place in Africana culture and in the aesthetic life of the nation. For the new generation, tapping is the foot version of the talking drum, a contemplative tool of the first order.

Tap dance as a secular contemplative practice came into my view at an Atlanta showing of the Broadway show, *Bring in 'Da Noise, Bring in 'Da Funk*. The show is a tap-dancing re-creation of the journey of the black community from Africa through the present day. I watched as the star of the show, Savion Glover, created a contemplative moment with his feet, not unlike the ring shout dancers of coastal Georgia. Glover is a wild and insubordinate tap dancer. I don't know what it means to have insubordinate feet, but he has them. Savion offers a defiant stomping—a wacky, counterintuitive, revolutionary/integrationist reverie. It is a dance that will not compromise with the reality of life struggles. There are no words; the silence is filled with the sound of his feet and the voluntary surrender of the audience to the moment.

As the audience watched, the familiarity of the sound invited them to enter a truly contemplative space. The clack of heel and toe against wood brought us back to another time, when hush harbors held the hopes and entreaties of a desperate people. In the dance that was like what I imagine David might have danced, where one sheds inhibitions rather than clothes, there was a suspension of the ordinary that exceeded the theatrical moment.

On stage Glover is introspective, according to writer Joan Acocella: "He is simply occupying a space of his own, which is different from ours. . . . Perhaps tap is meant to be this way, not a lot of things but just one thing, a product of deep and private thought."[14] Refusing to "skin or grin" in the style of minstrel performers who sullied the art for some African Americans, Glover simply puts it down, then taps the questions that have no answers, inviting us into the hypnotic rhythms that move us inward. After all is said and done, the objective rational thinking aspect of our human life is balanced by a rhythmic breathing and pulsating interiority.

Rapping a Contemplative Word

"What then did you expect when you unbound the gag that had muted those black mouths? that they would chant praises?"[15] In the beginning when rap was raw and new, rappers were equal-opportunity offenders. With the exception of their fan base, they irked all groups equally. The dominant culture was angered by their defiance and the open threat of retaliation against oppressive systems and the enforcers of those systems. Women disliked the misogyny; black communities were uncomfortable with the brash attitude and abrasive truth-telling. Like all musical genres, rap continues to evolve, but even as it finds more mainstream expressions, it remains a challenging artistic venue. What is most notable is that its emergence surprised its musical and political predecessors. After years of politically correct discourse and the studied attempt to assimilate or integrate, the next generation arrived with a chip on its collective shoulder and with a story to tell.

The ancestors must be laughing: How could we have forgotten so easily that prophets arise in every generation? While we recognized this truism in past generations, we did not expect this revolutionary art form in the younger generation that followed the Civil Rights Movement because of the context of their lives. Most of them grew up in the era of "opportunity," when Jim Crow was either dead or on life support. Some were born to parents who had some modicum of education, a place to live, and enough food to eat. Others grew up in the "'hood" exposed to drugs and violence, yet the potential for transcendence seemed to be the one sure legacy of the Civil Rights Movement. Although today's teens do not live with the level of fear that pervaded slavery, the displacements still haunt the community. Post-Traumatic Stress Disorder passed from generation to generation; poor health and broken families created a new sense of isolation. Although there is no way to quantify or comparatively assess suffering, one can decry its agenda. This is what rappers do through rhyme and chant.

Their moment of contemplation comes in the creation of the artistic expression of their social, religious, and political views.

The performance is the post-contemplative moment when they claim their identity and then witness in the poetry that taunts, tells, and terrorizes. Even more important, they reject the status quo through the exaggeration of utterance and dress. The witness to the older generation is that tucking your shirt in to appear neat and acceptable to mainstream society has not dismantled the oppressions. Many rappers as children were teased by classmates because they had to wear handed-down clothes that did not fit or clothes that were entirely too big, which their parents bought so that they would not grow out of them so quickly. Now all of those careful survival techniques are derided as the rappers strut in oversized clothes flashing their jewels (bling bling) as a mockery and embrace of superficial values.

Jon Michael Spencer calls rap messages "the insurrection of subjugated knowledges."[16] But where did they receive this knowledge? These children grew up watching television and the clear class divisions depicted there, but they also watched their parents try to assimilate or integrate. They watched despair increase in the underclass as the black middle class eschewed communal values in favor of inclusion in the dominant culture. Those of means and those without resented the choices made and used poetry and music to call the black community back to its purposes. But what is contemplative about their prophetically pragmatic message?

One could argue that they have been cloistered all of their lives right in the midst of dominant culture. Those who live in the 'hood do not have to retreat to an isolated area like the desert mothers and fathers to consider their lives; instead, they are isolated by boundaries of race, class, gender, and sexuality. They find no comfort in churches focused on upward mobility, college degrees, and suburban homes. As a consequence they have only the tenuous church connections ceded to them by kinship. Everyone who loves their "big mama" learned the stories of faith and eschatological hope, but the language did not describe their realities.

Rap offers an inverted reality structure that redefines what is naughty and what is nice. Like blues and jazz musicians before them, rappers speak of sex casually but value family relations.

Tupac Shakur's love song to his mother is unmatched for its honesty about her failings, yet there is an unabashed declaration of love. When one of his "homies" has a baby, Pac declares that "the little rodder" has all of the crew as daddies. Clearly, thug life does not interfere with filial attachment or communal commitment. In fact, in the film *Tupac: Resurrection* we are told that Pac realizes that he has to offer something positive to all of the "underclass" who now revere him. Using creative inversion techniques, he redefines "thug life" as self-empowerment. He encourages fans to invert the definition of "thug" through moral acts that prioritize the well-being of the community and the self-respect of the individual.

Inevitably rap's mainline social commentary found its way into the church, spawning Christian rappers who confound and redefine the boundaries between the sacred and secular. According to Spencer,

> The hip-hop gospelers have begun to redefine what ministry to the "sick and shut-in" should entail. They perceive the "sick" to be those who lack unity with and self-actualization within the black community because, genocidally, they are politically held down, socially split up, and psychologically cut off from the root of their Africanity. The "shut-in" are those who are held captive on the modern plantations of America's neo-colonialist slavocracy, namely the victims of economic exploitation, selective criminal prosecution, covert government harassment, civil terrorism, and personal and institutional racialism.[17]

Once again the gospel is being inculturated for a new generation. To reconsider your circumstances using the new perspectives of a new generation is a difficult and contemplative act. It is contemplative because it requires the recognition that the reality we grasp is not of our own making. Another generation has its hands to the plow: they will not engage the world as we did; they are singing a new song. "This 'new song' must be embraced and encouraged by the black church if the historic institution is ever to reclaim its relevance."[18] Through the rhythmic defiance of the young, we hear the word of the Lord.

While black churches and communities struggle for inclusion and celebrate the journey toward a particular configuration of liberation, young people have revised their lives and language structures to reflect clear differences in their personal and ecclesial orientation. I think that I understand at least some of these language revisions. I can hear the existentialist angst seeded throughout Tupac's rhetoric; I can feel hip-hop beats and relate to their syncopated Africana discourses of alienation and resistance. For me the links are apparent. I cannot hear Aretha Franklin without remembering Mahalia Jackson, cannot watch Savion Glover tap without a cultural recall of step dancers and ring shouters. But there is more: seeded within this reflexive engagement with history is a communal response to faith that has unique expressions in the church but also in the world that God so loves.

Contemplation is such an integral part of the human experience that it cannot be confined to designated sacred spaces. As noted by Ronald Rolheiser, the Protestant contemplative tradition is grounded in the experience of awe and wonder.

> God cannot be understood in concepts and the existence of God cannot be captured imaginatively or even felt in a possessive feeling, but [God] can be experienced, touched, and undergone. God cannot be thought, but God can be met. Through awe and wonder we experience God and there, as mystics have always stated, we understand more by not understanding than by understanding. In that posture we let God be God. In such a posture, too, we live in contemplation.[19]

Artistic Reflections

These artistic genres are contemplative because they ignite memories of the awe and wonder that we tend to discard after childhood. Art also carves pathways toward our inner isles of spirituality. When we decide to live in our heads only, we become isolated from the God who is closer than our next breath. To subject everything to rational analysis reduces the awe to ashes. The restoration of wonder is the beginning of the inward journey toward a God who people of faith aver is always waiting in the seeker's heart. For some the call to worship comes as joy spurts from jazz riffs, wonder thunders from tappers' feet, each riff and blues note is just slightly beyond our understanding. What a gift it is, this lack of understanding. Perhaps we are confounded so that we might always have much to contemplate.

Afterword
Toward a Future Together

> It is joy unspeakable and full of glory,
> Full of glory, full of glory
> It is joy unspeakable and full of glory
> Oh, the half has never yet been told.
> —Barney E. Warren, "Joy Unspeakable"

This song is a testimony about spiritual revival. Because the experience is profoundly transcendent, the lyrics can only attest to a joy beyond description. I introduced this book as a phenomenological inquiry into contemplative practices in the black church. Ultimately those practices only point to traces of experience and historical memory. It is a daunting but not impossible task to describe the indescribable. Song, dance, and ritual help. This is how Grant Wacker describes the joy that emerges out of spiritual revival: "And then there was joy—not necessarily happiness, a passing emotion—but joy, the quiet deep-seated conviction that one's life made sense."[1]

Does your life make sense? This is a difficult question to answer; I believe that we are only at the beginning of the process. First we have to be willing to raise the questions and begin the journey toward answers. From the beginning, Africana people in the diaspora have defined the sensibility of their lives within the context of struggle and resistance. We have begun to realize that while overt systematic oppression may be removed, we all bear the scars and traces of racism's collective demonic possession. And yet we must all go on, and we must all go on together as the people of God.

Our obsession with one another and with the question of who is or is not worthy of God's full embrace turns us from the pilgrimage toward the center of our hearts. It is in this place of prayerful repose that joy unspeakable erupts. This joy beckons us not as individual monastics but as a community. It is a joy that lives as comfortably in the shout as it does in silence. It is expressed in the diversity of personal spiritual disciplines and liturgical rituals.

Black church worship practices once encompassed a wide range of liturgical options. In the dance, shout, moan, or prayer the potential for contemplative meditation or ecstatic witness was available. As worship formats have conformed more closely to familiar entertainment patterns, we have lost rich and diverse liturgical resources. Praise teams are wonderful, recording-class choirs are great, but the price for so much professionalism may be the loss of genuine and unexpected expressions of joy unspeakable, of sorrow unfathomable, of the range of human emotions that speak to the diversity intrinsic to life. When the black church mimics the corporation, the deep solace of coming together is lost.

Time is of the essence when several services are back to back. Is there time to tarry, to wait for the Spirit to move? I am not expressing a desire to return to interminably long testimony services in which everyone is auditioning for the preacher's job. Instead this is a quiet plea for the bosom of the Old Ship of Zion. There weary sojourners could lay their heads, wipe a tear from their eyes, and wait on the Lord. We are embarking on a new millennium, and we are not healed. How shall we negotiate postmodernity without inner strength?

Even those who remain faithful church members suffer from devastated self-esteem, nihilism, and debilitating health issues. Since the intensity of these afflictions has not been assuaged by the ritual enactment of cathartic practices, I am suggesting a turn inward to face the inner conflicts and seeping psychic wounds that can no longer be ignored. One solution will not fit all. We are in need of all of our spiritual resources. Accordingly, as bell hooks suggests, we must seek an emancipatory spirituality, the soul's guiding light in the midst of collective blindness. This light has never left us. We need only make the contemplative turn to restore our inner sight.

In this book I have described the contemplative practices of the black church as a protective membrane that held the community in safety during the crisis of overt communal oppression and individual angst. According to leading cosmologist Brian Swimme, all of humankind needs to be held.[2] The universe has a method of doing that through such physical phenomena as gravity, the amniotic sac that holds us until birth, the atmospheric ozone layer that cradles the earth and protects it, the skin that we are in that keeps our innards from falling out, the air that we breathe that surrounds and envelops us.

According to Swimme, when we do not feel held, we create restrictions and rules to hold us and protect us from groundlessness.[3] In ways that are yet to be explored, the black church developed contemplative holding mechanisms that served just as well as cathartic options. We have forgotten how to pause and rest, how to care for and heal one another. We are in need of all of the membranes of faith that brought us through the tribulation.

This was not an easy book to write. The practices that I treasure as gifts handed down from loved ancestors are elusive. They cannot withstand the light of objective scrutiny for too long. The root women and dreamkeeping visionaries cannot explain why they know what they know. Even if they could, no scientist or theologian would be satisfied. Contemplative practices that run contrary to aesthetic and traditional expectations are just as difficult to justify. Still, this effort is necessary because Africana contemplative practices are historical and spiritual assets that must be reclaimed for the survival of the community.

Some of the rituals and nuances of contemplation in black church worship have been lost forever. If that is the case, we will need to begin a creative construction of worship options that restore the contemplative aspects of Africana faith and practice. Why? Because the retrieval of contemplative practices in black church worship and community life may be just the balm in Gilead that we have been seeking.

Joy unspeakable . . . full of glory, . . .
Oh, the half has never yet been told.

Notes

Introduction: An Unlikely Legacy

1. As I noted in the preface and will discuss fully in this chapter, the phrase "black church" is a symbolic/historical reference to worshipping communities who share a cultural legacy. The phrase transcends the usual denominational boundaries to include Protestant and Catholic practices that emerge from an "invisible institution" forged in crisis.

2. M. Shawn Copeland, "Foundations for Catholic Theology in an African American Context," in *Black and Catholic: The Challenge and Gift of Black Folk, Contributions of African American Experience and Thought to Catholic Theology*, ed. Jamie T. Phelps (Milwaukee: Marquette University Press, 1997).

3. Delores S. Williams, *Sisters in the Wilderness: The Challenge of Womanist God-Talk* (Maryknoll, N.Y.: Orbis, 1993), 206.

4. Moses Berry, "The Lost Heritage of African-Americans," in *An Unbroken Circle: Linking Ancient African-American Experience*, ed. Paisius Altschul (St. Louis: Brotherhood of St. Moses the Black, 1997), 65.

5. Howard Thurman, *The Centering Moment* (New York: Harper & Row, 1969).

6. Howard Thurman, "The Inward Sea," in *Meditations of the Heart* (1953; repr., Richmond, Ind.: Friends United, 1976), 28–29.

7. Ibid., 29.

8. Peter Berger and Thomas Luckmann, *The Social Construction of Reality* (New York: Anchor, 1990).

9. These indigenous expressions of wisdom and second sight also emerge in other ethnic cultures that include multiple realities in their sacred belief systems.

10. Patrick A. Kalilombe, "Spirituality in the African Perspective," in *Paths of African Theology*, ed. Rosino Gibellini (Maryknoll, N.Y.: Orbis, 1994), 124.

11. Martin Luther King Jr., *The Strength to Love* (New York: Harper & Row, 1963), excerpted in *Testament of Hope: The Essential Writings and Speeches of Martin Luther King, Jr.*, ed. James M. Washington (San Francisco: HarperSanFrancisco, 1991), 501, 502.

12. Ibid., 501–2.

13. Robert Orsi, *Lived Religion in America: Toward a History of Practices*, ed. David Hall (Princeton, N.J.: Princeton University Press, 1997), 11.

14. I am aware that whenever scholars attempt to make connections from the diaspora to the continent of Africa, questions arise as to the validity of the theory of "retentions." Within the context of slavery, this debate about the existence of cultural memory coalesced around the arguments of Melville Herskowitz and E. Franklin Frazier. Although this debate no longer fuels scholarly disagreement, new arguments rage about Afrocentricity and the contributions of Africana culture to the intellectual capital of classical societies (like Greece).

1. Contemplation: A Cultural and Spiritual History

1. Ernest E. Larkin, O.Carm., "Contemplative Prayer Forms Today: Are They Contemplation?" in *The Diversity of Centering Prayer*, ed. Gustave Reininger (New York: Continuum, 1989), 106, 107.

2. M. Basil Pennington, *Centering Prayer: Renewing an Ancient Christian Prayer Form* (New York: Doubleday, 1980), 31.

3. Ibid., 107.

4. C. S. Lewis, *Surprised by Joy: The Shape of My Early Life* (London: G. Bles, 1955), 22.

5. Howard Thurman, *Deep Is the Hunger* (New York: Harper, 1951), 15.

6. Howard Thurman, *Meditations of the Heart* (1953; repr., Richmond, Ind.: Friends United, 1976), 28.

7. Jürgen Moltmann, *The Spirit of Life: A Universal Affirmation*, trans. Margaret Kohl (Minneapolis: Fortress Press, 1992), 50.

8. Ibid., 48.

9. Thomas Keating, *Open Mind, Open Heart: The Contemplative Dimension of the Gospel* (New York: Continuum, 1999), 13.

10. William H. Shannon, *Thomas Merton's Paradise Journey: Writings on Contemplation* (Cincinnati: St. Anthony Messenger, 2000), 136.

11. Barbara A. Holmes, *Race and the Cosmos: An Invitation to View the World Differently* (Harrisburg, Pa.: Trinity Press International, 2002).

12. *An Unbroken Circle: Linking Ancient African Christianity to the African-American Experience*, ed. Paisius Altschul (St. Louis: Brotherhood of St. Moses the Black, 1997), 10, 11.

13. Ibid., 42.

14. Laura Swan, *The Forgotten Desert Mothers: Sayings, Lives, and Stories of Early Christian Women* (New York: Paulist, 2001), 8.

15. Ibid., 168.

16. Ibid., 25.

17. Judith L. Webb, "Protestant Sisterhood," 41, unpublished (Senior Seminar, McMaster Divinity College, Ontario, Canada, 1985). See also François Biot, *The Rise of Protestant Monasticism*, trans. W. J. Kerrigan (Dublin: Helicon, 1963), 120.

18. Conversation with Dr. Paul Dekar, May 5–10, 2004. Holy Transfiguration Community includes three lifestyles: the Cloister (about twenty-five family units), the Greater Community (about three hundred lay associates), and the Skete (a center in Melbourne, Australia, for prayer and contemplation).

19. There are approximately 25,000 lay associates (third-order), both Catholic and Protestant, in the United States.

20. Conversation with Dr. Waldo E. Knickerbocker Jr., Memphis Theological Seminary, April 2004.

21. Ibid. The pondering Mary is discussed more fully in chapter 5.

22. Randall C. Bailey, "Africans in Old Testament Poetry and Narratives," in *Stony the Road We Trod: African American Biblical Interpretation*, ed. Cain Hope Felder (Minneapolis: Fortress Press, 1991), 166.

23. Rosino Gibellini, ed., "Africans Theologians Wonder and Make Some Proposals," in *Paths of African Theology* (Maryknoll, N.Y.: Orbis, 1994), 4, quoting Roland Oliver and J. D. Fage, *Breve storia dell' Africa* (A Short History of Africa), 4th ed. rev. (Turin: Einaudi, 1974), 140.

24. Gibellini, "African Theologians Wonder," 5, quoting Louis-Vincent Thomas and René Luneau in *La Terre africaine et ses religions* (Paris: Larousse, 1975), 327–28.

25. Stephen G. Ray Jr., "Cartographies of Race: Mapping a Landscape of Exclusion," Black History Lectures, February 29, 2004, Memphis Theological Seminary.

26. William R. Jones, *Is God a White Racist? A Preamble to Black Theology* (Boston: Beacon, 1998), xv.

27. Anthony B. Pinn, *Why, Lord? Suffering and Evil in Black Theology* (New York: Continuum, 1995).

28. Josiah Ulysses Young III, *Dogged Strength within the Veil: Africana Spirituality and the Mysterious Love of God* (Harrisburg, Pa.: Trinity Press International, 2003), 7.

29. Ibid.

30. William Johnston, *Mystical Theology: The Science of Love* (Maryknoll, N.Y.: Orbis, 1998), 214.

31. Keating, *Open Mind, Open Heart*, 6.

32. Paisius Altschul, "African Monasticism: Its Influence on the Rest of the World," in *An Unbroken Circle*, 26–43.

33. Ibid., 27.

34. Charles H. Long, *Significations: Signs, Symbols, and Images in the Interpretation of Religion* (Philadelphia: Fortress Press, 1986), 62.

35. Long, *Significations*, 61.

36. Ibid., 60.

37. Max Picard, *The World of Silence*, Humanist Library, trans. Stanley Godman (Chicago: Regner, 1952), 5, 11.

38. Ibid., 25.

2. Retrieving Lost Legacies: Contemplation in West Africa

1. Theo Sundermeier, *The Individual and Community in African Traditional Religions* (Piscataway, N.J.: Transaction, 1998), 15.

2. Robert C. Williams, "Ritual, Drama, and God in Black Religion: Theological and Anthropological Views," *Theology Today* 41/4 (January 1985): 435.

3. Albert Raboteau, "Afterword," in *An Unbroken Circle: Linking Ancient African Christianity to the African-American Experience*, ed. Paisius Altschul (St. Louis: Brotherhood of St. Moses the Black, 1997), 162.

4. Ibid.

5. Ibid., 163.

6. According to Kathleen O'Brien Wicker, Mami Water is "the name applied by Africans to a class of female and male water divinities." It is a syncretized projection of African, European, and Indian origin. "Mami Water in African Religion and Spirituality," in *African Spirituality: Forms Meanings and Expressions*, ed. Jacob K. Olupona (New York: Crossroad, 2000), 199.

7. Wicker, "Mami Water," 213, citing unpublished paper, "Toward a History of Global Religion(s) in the Twentieth Century: Parachristian Sightings from an Interdisciplinary Asianist," Sixteenth Annual Univer-

sity Lecture in Religion, Arizona State University, Department of Religious Studies, p. 6.

8. Conversations with Dr. Marcel Oyono, University of Memphis.

9. Yoruban culture is an urban, artistic, and ancient culture with large concentrations of people in southwestern Nigeria.

10. Robert Farris Thompson, *Flash of the Spirit: African and Afro-American Art and Philosophy* (New York: Vintage, 1984), 9.

11. Olu Taiwo, "Music, Art, and Movement among the Yoruba," in *Indigenous Religions: A Companion*, ed. Graham Harvey (New York: Cassell, 2000), 173–89; 177.

12. Charles S. Finch III, *The Star of Deep Beginnings: The Genesis of African Science and Technology* (Decatur, Ga.: Khenti, 2001), 264.

13. Taiwo, "Music, Art, and Movement," 176.

14. Ibid., quoting van Nieuwenhuijze, "The Simplicity of Complexity," unpublished paper at the Fourteenth World Congress of Sociology, Montreal, 1998.

15. Williams, "Ritual, Drama, and God," 436.

16. Taiwo, "Music, Art, and Movement," 179.

17. Kabir Edmund Helminski, *Living Presence: A Sufi Way to Mindfulness and the Essential Self* (New York: Tarcher/Perigee, 1992).

18. Allan D. Austin, *African Muslims in Antebellum America: Transatlantic Stories and Spiritual Struggles* (New York: Routledge, 1997), 22.

19. Jay Kinney, "Sufism Comes West: An Introduction to Sufism," *Hidden Wisdom: A Guide to the Western Inner Traditions* (New York: Penguin/Arkana, 1999).

20. Other mystical leaders of the movement include Hasan al-Basri (624–728), Rai'ah al-Adawiya (d. 801), and al-Hallaj (857–922). Movements began with spiritual leaders and students, who were followed by the development of religious orders.

21. Kinney, "Sufism," 6.

22. William C. Chittick, "Rumi and the Mawlawiyyah," in *Islamic Spirituality: Manifestations*, ed. Seyyed Hossein Nasr (New York: Crossroad, 1997).

23. Louis Brenner, "Sufism in Africa," in *African Spirituality: Forms, Meanings, and Expressions*, World Spirituality 3, ed. Jacob K. Olupona (New York : Crossroad, 2000), 327.

24. Abdur-Rahman Ibrahim Doi, "Sufism in Africa," in *Islamic Spirituality*, 290–303; 291.

25. Brenner, "Sufism in Africa," 324, 327.

26. Ibid., 324.

27. Ibid., 346, 347.

28. Ibid., 347.

29. Mervyn Hiskett, *The Sword of Truth: The Life and Times of Shehu Usuman dan Fodio* (New York: Oxford University Press, 1973), 64f., cited in Lamin Sanneh's *Piety and Power: Muslims and Christians in West Africa* (Maryknoll, N.Y.: Orbis, 1996), 55.

30. Graham Harvey, "Introduction," in *Indigenous Religions*, 3, 7–12.

31. Jean-Marc Ela, *My Faith as an African* (Maryknoll, N.Y.: Orbis, 1995), 40.

32. Victor Turner and Edith L. B. Turner, *Image and Pilgrimage in Christian Culture* (New York: Columbia University Press, 1978), 249.

33. YaYa Diallo and Mitchell Hall, *The Healing Drum: African Wisdom Teachings* (Rochester, Vt.: Destiny, 1989), 67.

34. Graham Harvey, *Readings in Indigenous Religion* (London: Continuum, 2002), 133.

35. Ela, *My Faith*, 41.

36. Ibid.

37. Oludare Olajubu, "African Culture and Science in Dialogue," unpublished paper presented at the African Conference on Science and Religion, University of Ilorin, Nigeria (October 19–24, 2001), p. 8.

38. Malidome Somé, *The Healing Wisdom of Africa: Finding Life Purpose through Nature, Ritual, and Community* (New York: Penguin Putnam, 1999), 92.

39. Ibid., 93.

40. Ibid.

41. Olajubu, "African Culture and Science," 10.

42. John S. Mbiti, *African Religions and Philosophy*, 2nd ed. (Portsmouth, N.H.: Heinemann, 1990), 109.

43. Robert E. Hood, *Must God Remain Greek? Afro Cultures and God-Talk* (Minneapolis: Fortress Press, 1990), 161.

44. Mbiti, *African Religions*, 146.

45. Kofi Asare Opoku, "Death and Immortality in the African Religious Heritage," in *Death and Immortality in the Religions of the World*, ed. Paul and Linda Badham (New York: Paragon, 1987), 15.

46. Babalawo Kolawole Ositola, "On Ritual Performance: A Practitioner's View," *The Drama Review* 32/2 (1988): 31–41.

47. Georges Niangoran-Bouah, "Talking Drum: A Traditional African Instrument of Liturgy and of Mediation with the Sacred," in *African Traditional Religions in Contemporary Society* (New York: Paragon, 1991), 86.

48. Ibid.

49. Ibid.

50. Ibid., 85.

51. Ibid., 87.

52. W. Komla Amoaku, "Toward a Definition of Traditional African Music: A Look at the Ewe of Ghana," in *More than Drumming: Essays on African and Afro-Latin American Music and Musicians*, ed. Irene V. Jackson (Westport, Conn.: Greenwood, 1985), 37.

53. Dorian Friedman, "Drumming to the Rhythms of Life," *U.S. News & World Report* 122/22 (June 9, 1997): 17.

54. *African Roots/American Cultures: Africa in the Creation of the Americas*, ed. Sheila S. Walker (Lanham, Md.: Rowman & Littlefield, 2001), 37.

55. Kofi Agawu, *African Rhythm: A Northern Ewe Perspective* (Cambridge: Cambridge University Press, 1995), 7.

56. Ibid.

57. Daphne D. Harrison, "Aesthetic and Social Aspects of Music in African Ritual," in *More Than Drumming*, 62.

58. Taiwo, "Music, Art, and Movement," 174–75, 183–88, citing his article "The 'Return Beat,'" in *The Virtual Embodied: Presence/Practice/Technology*, ed. John Wood (London: Routledge, 1998), 157–67.

59. Taiwo, "Music, Art, and Movement," 188.

60. This phrase is taken from the title of a Countee Cullen (1903–1946) poem.

3. Every Shut Eye Ain't Sleep: The Inner Life during Slavery

1. Howard Thurman, *Deep River and the Negro Spiritual Speaks of Life and Death* (Richmond, Ind.: Friends United, 1975), 29.

2. Lamine Kebe quoted in Allan D. Austin, *African Muslims in Antebellum America* (New York: Routledge, 1997), 11.

3. Cited in Anthony B. Pinn, *Terror and Triumph: The Nature of Black Religion* (Minneapolis: Fortress Press, 2003), 28.

4. Pinn, *Terror and Triumph*, 35.

5. Arnold van Gennep, *The Rites of Passage* (Chicago: University of Chicago Press, 1960).

6. Victor Turner, *The Ritual Process* (Chicago: Aldine, 1969), 94–96.

7. Victor Turner, *Dramas, Fields, and Metaphors* (Ithaca, N.Y.: Cornell University Press, 1974), 259.

8. Mihaly Csikszentmihalyi, "Play and Intrinsic Rewards," *Journal of Humanistic Psychology* 15 (1975): 41–63.

9. Mihaly Csikszentmihalyi, *Beyond Boredom and Anxiety: The Experience of Play in Work and Games* (San Francisco: Jossey Bass, 1975), 11–38.

10. William Stringfellow, *The Politics of Spirituality: Spirituality and The Christian Life*, ed. Richard H. Bell (Philadelphia: Westminster, 1984), 89, 90.

11. Eric Cassell, *The Nature of Suffering* (New York: Oxford University Press, 1991), 24, 25.

12. Elaine Scarry, *The Body in Pain: The Making and Unmaking of the World* (New York: Oxford University Press, 1985), 49.

13. James F. Keenan, S.J., "Suffering and the Christian Tradition," *The Yale Journal for Humanities in Medicine* (March 20, 2002); available at http://info.med.yale.edu/intmed/hummed/yjhm/index.html.

14. James A. Noel, "Call and Response: The Meaning of the Moan and Significance of the Shout in Black Worship," *Reformed Liturgy & Music* 28/2 (spring 1994): 72–76; 73.

15. Ibid.

16. Ibid.

17. *The Interesting Narrative of the Life of Olaudah Equiano*, 1789.

18. Ibid.

19. Robert W. Harms, *The Diligent: A Voyage through the Worlds of the Slave Trade* (New York: Basic, 2002).

20. Olly Wilson, "It Don't Mean a Thing If It Ain't Got That Swing: The Relationship between African and African American Music," in *African Roots/American Cultures: Africa in the Creation of the Americas*, ed. Sheila S. Walker (Lanham, Md.: Rowman and Littlefield, 2001), 158.

21. Sterling Stuckey, "Christian Conversion and the Challenge of Dance," in *Choreographing History*, ed. Susan Foster (Bloomington: Indiana University Press, 1995), 54–65; 56.

22. Interview with Horation J. Eden, 1923, Arkansas, in *Slave Testimony: Two Centuries of Letters, Speeches, Interviews, and Autobiographies*, ed. John W. Blassingame (Baton Rouge: Louisiana State University Press, 1977), 631–32.

23. Dwight N. Hopkins, *Down, Up, and Over: Slave Religion and Black Theology* (Minneapolis: Fortress Press, 2000), 102.

24. The account of Stephen Dickenson Jr., in *Slave Testimony*, 690.

25. Blassingame, *Slave Testimony*, 502.

26. "Statement of a Slave (William Davis) during a Meeting in Dr. Cheever's Church," in *Slave Testimony*, 170.

27. Thurman, *Deep River*, 40, 41.

28. Ibid., 42.

29. Ibid., 42.

30. William Johnston, *Mystical Theology: The Science of Love* (Maryknoll, N.Y.: Orbis, 1995), 4.

31. Moses Berry, "Lost Heritage of African-Americans," in *Unbroken Circle: Linking Ancient African-American Experience*, ed. Paisius Altschul (St. Louis: Brotherhood of St. Moses the Black, 1997), 67.

32. Arthur Deikman, "Deautomatization and the Mystic Experience," *Psychiatry* 29 (1966): 324–38.

33. Cited in Henry H. Mitchell, *Black Belief: Folk Beliefs of Blacks in America and West Africa* (New York: Harper & Row, 1975), 102.

34. *Born in Slavery: Slave Narratives from the Federal Writers' Project, 1936–1938* (Washington, D.C.: Library of Congress, 1941), 49.

35. This quotation bears no name or reference to state or location; cited in Mitchell, *Black Belief*, 101, citing George P. Rawick, *The American Slave: A Composite Autobiography*, vol. 1: *From Sundown to Sunup* (Westport, Conn.: Greenwood, 1972).

36. Hopkins, *Down, Up, and Over*, 141.

37. Doug Adams, "Communal Dance Forms and Consequences in Biblical Worship," in *Dance as Religious Studies*, ed. Doug Adams and Diane Apostolos-Cappadona (New York: Crossroad, 1990) 38.

38. Ibid., 39, 40.

39. Robert Farris Thompson, "An Aesthetic of the Cool: West African Dance," *African Forum* 2/2 (1966): 85–102.

40. Ann-Janine Morey, "Toni Morrison and the Color of Life," *Christian Century* (November 16, 1988): 1039.

41. Lorenzo Dow Turner, *Africanisms in the Gullah Dialect* (repr., Ann Arbor: University of Michigan Press, 1949), 202.

42. Howard Farrar, "The African Roots of Steppin'," paper presented in the History Department of Virginia Polytechnic Institute and State University.

43. Art Rosenbaum, *Shout Because You're Free: The African American Ring Shout Tradition in Coastal Georgia* (Athens: University of Georgia Press, 1998), 11.

44. David D. Daniels, "The Cultural Renewal of Slave Religion: Charles Price Jones and the Emergence of the Holiness Movement in Mississippi," Ph.D. dissertation (Union Theological Seminary, New York, 1992), 85.

45. Tom F. Driver, *Liberating Rites: Understanding the Transformative Power of Ritual* (Boulder: Westview, 1991), 66.

46. Ibid.

47. Blassingame, *Slave Testimony*, 169; "Escape and Capture of Stephen Pembroke, Related by Himself," *New York Tribune* (July 18, 1854).

48. Thurman, *Deep River*, 42, 43.

4. Come Ye Disconsolate:
Contemplation in Black Church Congregational Life

1. Paul Dekar, *Holy Boldness: Practices of an Evangelistic Lifestyle* (Macon, Ga.: Smyth & Helwys, 2004), 73.

2. William D. Watley, *Singing the Lord's Song in a Strange Land: The African American Churches and Ecumenism* (Geneva: WCC Publications, 1993), 19.

3. James H. Cone, "Sanctification, Liberations and Black Worship," *Theology Today* 35/2 (July 1978): 139–51; 139.

4. Phrase from the Negro national anthem "Lift Every Voice and Sing" written by James Weldon Johnson, music written by his brother John R. Johnson, 1899.

5. Thomas Merton, *Seeds of Contemplation* (New York: New Directions, 1961), 136.

6. Cone, "Sanctification, Liberations and Black Worship," 140.

7. William James, *Varieties of Religious Experience* (New York: Modern Library, 1919), 245.

8. Medjugorje is the site in Bosnia-Herzegovina where believers say the Virgin Mary has made several appearances, the first in 1981.

9. James, *Varieties of Religious Experience*, 242ff.

10. The informal references to high and low churches denote formality or the lack thereof. Although these categories are not rigid, high churches are noted for their formality, structure, and adherence to tradition. Low churches tend to focus on the experiential and the solicitation of God's active presence.

11. Annie Dillard, *Holy the Firm* (New York: Harper & Row, 1977), 59.

12. Jyoti Sahi, "The Body in Search of Identity," in *Liturgy and the Body*, ed. Louis Chauvet and François Kabasele Lumbala (Maryknoll, N.Y.: Orbis, 1995), 91.

13. Doug Adams, "Communal Dance Forms and Consequences in Biblical Worship," in *Dance as Religious Studies*, ed. Doug Adams and Diane Apostolos-Cappadona (New York: Crossroad, 1990), 37.

14. Ibid., citing Chr. Bromel, *Fest-Tantze der ersten Christen* (Jena, 1703), English translation in E. Louis Backman, *Religious Dances in the Christian Church and in Popular Medicine*, trans. E. Classen (London: Allen & Unwin, 1952), 31.

15. Glen Hinson, *Fire in My Bones: Transcendence and the Holy Spirit in African American Gospel*, Contemporary Ethnography (Philadelphia: University of Pennsylvania Press, 2000), 254, 255.

16. Ibid., 257; 365, n. 28. The pastor of this church, Rev. Harris, keeps copies of the prophecies. The quoted passage was uttered by Sister Vera Turner and dated October 26, 1992.

17. James Albert Ukawsaw Gronniosaw, *A Narrative of the Most Remarkable Particulars in the Life of James Albert Ukawsaw Gronniosaw, An African Prince* (Glasgow: David Robertson, Tronsgate, 1840), 23; also cited in Love Henry Whelchel Jr.'s *Hell without Fire: Conversion in Slave Religion* (Nashville: Abingdon, 2002), 41, 42.

18. Albert J. Raboteau, *Canaan Land: A Religious History of African Americans* (Oxford: Oxford University Press, 1999), 45, 46.

19. Hinson, *Fire in My Bones*, 319, 320.

20. Ibid., 320.

21. Ibid., 323.

22. Ibid., quoting Dorothy Scarborough, *On the Trail of Negro Folk-Songs* (Hatboro, Pa.: Folklore Associates, 1963), 14–16.

23. Marquetta L. Goodwine, *The Legacy of Ibo Landing: Gullah Roots of African American Culture* (Atlanta: Clarity, 1998), 96.

24. Joseph M. Murphy, *Working the Spirit: Ceremonies of the African Diaspora* (Boston: Beacon, 1994), 150.

25. "There Is a River," *This Far by Faith: African-American Spiritual Journeys*, video docudrama by Henry Hampton, Georgia Public Broadcasting, June 9, 2003.

26. Ibid.

27. See Dwight N. Hopkins, *Down, Up, and Over: Slave Religion and Black Theology* (Minneapolis: Fortress Press, 2000), 122, 123.

28. Hinson, *Fire in My Bones*, 210.

29. Ibid., 213.

30. David Daniels, "Until the Power of the Lord Comes Down: African American Pentecostal Spirituality and Tarrying," in *Contemporary Spiritualities: Social and Religious Contexts* (New York: Continuum, 2001), 173–91; 178.

31. Ibid., 184.

5. Joy Comes in the Morning: Contemplative Themes in African American Biblical Interpretation

1. Dennis Fischman, "Midrash as Political Practice," *The Shalom Center*, http://www.shalomctr.org/index.cfm/action/read/section/natr/article/torah47.html.

2. Ibid.

3. Cheryl Kirk-Duggan, "Let My People Go! Threads of Exodus in African American Narratives," in *Yet with a Steady Beat: Contemporary U.S. Afrocentric Biblical Interpretation*, Semeia Studies 42, ed. Randall C. Bailey (Atlanta: Society of Biblical Literature, 2003), 125.

4. *TANAK, the Holy Scripture: The New JPS Translation according to the Traditional Hebrew Text* (Philadelphia: Jewish Publication Society, 1985).

5. Walter Brueggemann, *Theology of the Old Testament: Testimony, Dispute, and Advocacy* (Minneapolis: Fortress Press, 1997), 357.

6. Tammy R. Williams, "Is There a Doctor in the House? Reflections on the Practice of Healing in African American Churches," in *Practicing Theology: Beliefs and Practices in Christian Life*, ed. Miroslav Volf and Dorothy C. Bass (Grand Rapids: Eerdmans, 2002), 111.

7. Sabine Jell-Bahlsen, "The Lake Goddess Uhammiri/Ogbuide: The Female Side of the Universe in Igbo Cosmology," in *African Spirituality: Forms, Meanings, and Expressions*, ed. Jacob K. Olupona (New York: Crossroad, 2000), 40.

8. Thomas Merton, *New Seeds of Contemplation* (Norfolk, Conn.: New Directions, 1961), 250.

9. John W. Waters, "Who Was Hagar?" in *Stony the Road We Trod: African American Biblical Interpretation*, ed. Cain Hope Felder (Minneapolis: Fortress Press, 1991), 198.

10. Ibid., 199 n. 17. Waters notes that Manoa the Danite in Judg. 13:12 also has a theophany but does not receive the commitment of descendants and land.

11. Phyllis Trible, *Texts of Terror: Literary-Feminist Readings of Biblical Narratives*, Overtures to Biblical Theology (Philadelphia: Fortress Press, 1984), 18; Delores S. Williams, *Sisters in the Wilderness: The Challenge of Womanist God-Talk* (Maryknoll, N.Y.: Orbis, 1993), 23.

12. Pierre Teilhard de Chardin, *On Love* (London: Collins, 1967), 73.

13. Bonnie J. Miller-McLemore, "Pondering All These Things: Mary and Motherhood," in *Blessed One: Protestant Perspectives on Mary*, ed. Beverly Roberts Gaventa and Cynthia Rigby (Louisville: Westminster John Knox, 2002), 105.

14. Ibid., 128, 129.

15. Walter Brueggemann, *Reverberations of Faith: A Theological Handbook of Old Testament Themes* (Louisville: Westminster John Knox, 2002), 119.

16. Howard Thurman, *Temptations of Jesus* (Richmond, Ind.: Friends United, 1962), 60.

17. Ibid., 61.

18. Antonious Conner, "Overview of Ancient Christianity in Africa," in *An Unbroken Circle: Linking Ancient African Christianity to the African-American Experience*, ed. Paisius Altschul (St. Louis: Brotherhood of St. Moses the Black, 1997), 6.

19. Stephanie Buckhanon Crowder, *Simon of Cyrene: A Case of Roman Conscription*, Studies in Biblical Literature 46 (New York: Peter Lang, 2002), 95–98.

6. Ain't Gonna Let Nobody Turn Us Around: Contemplation, Activism, and Praxis

1. Victor Turner, *The Ritual Process: Structure and Anti-Structure* (Chicago: University of Chicago, 1969).

2. Marsha Sinetar, *A Way without Words: A Guide for Spiritually Emerging Adults* (New York: Paulist, 1992), 33.

3. James A. Noel, "Contemplation and Social Action in Afro-American Spirituality," *Pacific Theological Review* 22/1 (fall 1988): 18–28; 25.

4. Ibid.

5. *The Simone Weil Reader*, ed. George A. Panichas (New York: McKay, 1977), 457.

6. Ronald L. Grimes, *Reading, Writing, and Ritualizing: Ritual in Fictive Liturgical and Public Places* (Washington, D.C.: Pastoral, 1993), 63.

7. Ibid., 64.

8. Ibid., 66.

9. Ibid., 65.

10. Victor Turner, *From Ritual to Theatre: The Human Seriousness of Play* (New York: Performing Arts Journal Publications, 1982), 113, 114.

11. I have fully documented the details of my experience in Selma in *Race and the Cosmos: An Invitation to View the World Differently* (Harrisburg, Pa.: Trinity Press International, 2002).

12. Rabbi Arthur Waskow, Shalom Institute, Fortieth Anniversary of the March on Washington, CSPAN, August 23, 2003.

13. Henri J. M. Nouwen, *Reaching Out: The Three Movements of the Spiritual Life* (New York: Doubleday, 1986), 153.

14. Ibid.

15. "BU Yesterday," *B. U. Bridge* 7/19 (February 13, 2004); available at www.bu.edu/bridge.

16. Flora Wilson Bridges, *Resurrection Song: African-American Spirituality* (Maryknoll, N.Y.: Orbis, 2001), 100, quoting Kay Mills, *This Little Light of Mine: The Life of Fannie Lou Hamer* (New York: Dutton, 1993), 17.

17. Rosetta E. Ross, *Witnessing and Testifying: Black Women, Religion, and Civil Rights* (Minneapolis: Fortress Press, 2003), 93.

18. Bridges, *Resurrection Song*, 102.

19. Conversation with Virginia Gray Adams, Lived Theology and Civil Courage Conference, Charlottesville, Virginia, June 12–14, 2002.

20. Remarks of Andrew Young, at the funeral of Fannie Lou Hamer, quoted in Lynne Olson, *Freedom's Daughters: The Unsung Heroines of the Civil Rights Movement from 1830 to 1970* (New York: Scribner, 2001), 394.

21. Martin Luther King Jr., *The Strength to Love* (New York: Harper & Row, 1963), excerpted in *A Testament of Hope: The Essential Writings and Speeches of Martin Luther King, Jr.*, ed. James M. Washington (San Francisco: HarperSanFrancisco, 1991), 515.

22. Frank A. Thomas, "Renewing Your Yes," sermon given at Mississippi Boulevard Church, Palm Sunday, April 4, 2004.

23. King, "An Experiment in Love," in *A Testament of Hope*, 19.

24. King, "I See the Promised Land," in *A Testament of Hope*, 286.

25. Rosa Parks with Gregory J. Reed, *Quiet Strength: The Faith, the Hope and the Heart of a Woman Who Changed a Nation* (Grand Rapids: Zondervan, 1994), 23–24.

26. The Highlander Folk School (now Highlander Center) was founded in 1932 by Myles Horton as a grassroots education institution. Many activists in the Civil Rights Movement attended leadership training and other workshops there.

27. Olson, *Freedom's Daughters*, 109.

28. Howard Thurman, *With Head and Heart: The Autobiography of Howard Thurman* (New York: Harcourt Brace Jovanovich, 1979), 265.

29. Sue Bailey Thurman married Howard Thurman on June 12, 1932, two years after the death of his first wife, Kate. Sue was born on August 3, 1903, and attended a school in Washington D.C. run by Nannie Helen Burroughs. She was also educated at the Lucretia Mott School, Spelman Seminary, and finally Oberlin College. When she met Howard, she was a music instructor at Hampton Institute. She was the founding editor of the *AfraAmerican Woman's Journal*, which was the official journal of the National Council of Negro Women. In 1949 she published *Pioneers of Negro Origin*. She died on Christmas Day in 1996 at the age of ninety-three.

30. Michele N-K Collison, "Resurrecting the Thurman Legacy for the Next Millennium," *Black Issues in Higher Education* (November 11, 1999): 24–25; 25.

31. Howard Thurman, *The Luminous Darkness* (New York: McGraw-Hill, 1964), 22–23.

32. Alex Haley, *The Autobiography of Malcolm X* (New York: Grove, [1964] 1965), 9.

33. bell hooks, *Yearning: Race, Gender, and Cultural Politics* (Boston: South End, 1990), 80.

34. Ibid., 83.

35. Michael Eric Dyson, *Making Malcolm: The Myth and Meaning of Malcolm X* (New York: Oxford University Press, 1995), 141.

7. At the Crossroads:
Secular Reclamations of the Contemplative Life

1. Teresa L. Reed, *The Holy Profane: Religion in Black Popular Music* (Lexington: University of Kentucky Press, 2003), 146.

2. Teddy Pendergrass and Patricia Romanowski, *Truly Blessed* (New York: Putnam, 1998), 30.

3. Reed, *The Holy Profane*, 91.

4. Ibid., 60.

5. William Dean, *The American Spiritual Culture: And the Invention of Jazz, Football, and the Movies* (New York: Continuum, 2002), 121.

6. Ibid., 118.

7. Ibid.

8. V. Sue Zabel, "Gifts of the Spirit . . . and All That Jazz," Installation Sermon, Wesley Theological Seminary, May 2, 2002.

9. "All That Jazz: Reflections on the Death of Pastor John Gensel of St. Peter's Lutheran Church in New York," *Christian Century* (March 18, 1998).

10. Alain Locke, ed., *The Negro and His Music: Negro Art, Past and Present*, Afro-American Culture Series (1936; repr., New York: Arno, 1969), 31, 34.

11. Ibid., 79.

12. *Alain Locke: Reflections on a Modern Renaissance Man*, ed. Russell J. Linnemann (Baton Rouge: University of Louisiana Press, 1982), 116.

13. Locke, *The Negro and His Music*, 90.

14. Joan Acocella, "Taking Steps: Savion Glover at the Joyce Theatre," *The New Yorker* (January 12, 2004): 75, 78.

15. Jean-Paul Sartre, *Black Orpheus*, quoted in Jon Michael Spencer's " Rhapsody in Black: Utopian Aspirations," *Theology Today* 48/4 (January 1992): 444–51; 446.

16. Ibid., 447.

17. Spencer, "Rhapsody," 450.

18. Ibid.

19. Ronald Rohlheiser, *The Shattered Lantern: Rediscovering a Felt Presence of God* (New York: Crossroad, 2001), 117.

Afterword: Toward a Future Together

1. Grant Wacker, *Heaven Below: Early Pentecostals and American Culture* (Cambridge: Harvard University Press, 2001), 67.

2. Conversations with Brian Swimme at the Sophia Wisdom Center summer conference, "Race and the Cosmos," Holy Names College, Oakland, California, June 2002.

3. Ibid.

Index

and history of contemplation,
42, 44–46
hush arbors and, 83–84
slavery and, 79, 83–84
See also lament
Simon of Cyrene, 134–35
slavery, 68–89
auction blocks and, 76–79
communal responses to suffering, 71, 80–82
and creation of crisis communities, 76
and crisis contemplation, 69,
73
dance and, 75–76, 84–86
griosh and African ritual,
119–21
hush arbors and, 82–84, 120
laments and, 75–76, 78–79
the moan and new spiritual
vocabulary, 72, 73–75, 88
narratives from, 74, 77, 78,
79, 83
on the plantations, 80–84
ring shouts (dances) and,
84–86, 101–2
and salvific specificity, 80
silence and, 79, 83–84
the slaver's whip, 86–87
See also Middle Passage
social justice movements, 20–21,
138–68
activism, 140, 142–43
and Africana community,
140–41, 151–52
civil rights marches, 143–46
civil rights marches and debutante balls, 149–52
and power sources, 140–43
and conflicting messages of

black church, 147–52
creation of social justice communities, 139, 140, 146–47
Fannie Lou Hamer and,
153–57
and the institutional black
church, 140, 147–52
Martin Luther King Jr. and,
157–61
Malcolm X and, 165–68
Rosa Parks and, 161–63
public mystics and, 152–68
and reclamation of Africana
heritage, 141
and spiritual aspects of community, 151–52
suffering and redemption in,
141–42
Howard Thurman and,
163–65
Soelle, Dorothee, 24
Somé, Malidome, 59–60
Spencer, Jon Michael, 180, 181
Stringfellow, William, 71–72
Stuckey, Sterling, 75
suffering
and blues music, 173–74
the moan and, 72, 73–75, 80
and new spiritual vocabulary,
73–75, 88
redemption and, 141–42
slavery and, 71–72, 80–82
Sufi spirituality, 54–56
Swan, Laura, 35
Swimme, Brian, 186

Taiwo, Olu, 52–53, 54, 66
tap dancing, 176–78
Teresa of Avila, Saint, 36
Tertullian, 38, 40

CPSIA information can be obtained at www.ICGtesting.com
Printed in the USA
LVOW101236020213

318299LV00006B/168/P

9 780800 636432